HOKUSAI

J · HILLIER

HOKUSAI

PAINTINGS · DRAWINGS

AND WOODCUTS

PHAIDON

Phaidon Press Limited, Littlegate House, St Ebbe's Street, Oxford
Published in the United States of America by E. P. Dutton, New York

First published 1955
Third edition 1978

ISBN 0 7148 1833 X (hardback)
ISBN 0 7148 1834 8 (paperback)
Library of Congress Catalog Card Number: 78–50628

Printed in Great Britain by Burgess & Son Ltd, Abingdon

Acknowledgements

Author and publisher are much indebted to the following private collectors and museum authorities for permission to reproduce prints, paintings and drawings in their possession: Dr. Walter Amstutz, Männedorf, Switzerland (Pls. III, VI); Mme Berès, Paris (tailpieces on p. 133 and p. 134); the Museum of Fine Arts, Boston, Mass. (Figs. 14, 78); Bristol City Art Gallery (Pl. XV); Mr. Nathan Chaikin, Vendhôme, Switzerland (tailpiece on p.11); the Art Institute, Chicago (Figs. 17, 20, 28, 30, 31); the Chester Beatty Library, Dublin (Pls. IX, XVII); the Wadsworth Atheneum, Hartford, Conn. (Figs. 7, 16); Hakone Gallery, Japan (Figs. 75, 81, 95); the Trustees of the British Museum, London (Pls. I, IV, V, VII, VIII, X, XII, XIII, XIV, XVI, XVIII, Figs. 5, 6, 9, 11–13, 15, 18, 19, 21–3, 25, 29, 32, 34, 36–9, 42–50, 51, 53, 56–69, 71–2, 74, 77, 79, 80, 82–4, 88–91, 94, 96–9, 101–5, 109–15); the Victoria and Albert Museum, London (Figs. 8, 24, 52, 86); the Bibliothèque Nationale, Paris (Figs. 1, 2, 27); the Musée Guimet, Paris (Pl. XI, Fig. 70); the Louvre, Paris (Fig. 116); Tokyo National Museum (Fig. 76); and the Smithsonian Institution, Freer Gallery of Art, Washington, D.C. (Figs. 85, 87, 92, 93). Plate II and Figs. 3, 4, 10, 26, 33, 40, 41, 54, 55, 73, 100, 106–8 and the illustrations on p. 8 and p. 129 are from originals in the author's collection.

The Author has a further debt to record to his friends Mr. B. W. Robinson, formerly of the Victoria and Albert Museum, and Dr. Richard Lane of Kyoto, Japan, for much valuable assistance in regard to the Japanese language and in reading his typescript, and to Mr. Basil Gray, Keeper of Oriental Antiquities in the British Museum, and Professor Bowie, of Indiana University, for helpful suggestions in selecting drawings for reproduction; and thankfully expresses his gratitude to his wife for having, among all her other accomplishments, the virtues of the perfect secretary.

CONTENTS

PREFACE

IN the twenty-three years since this book first appeared there has been widespread and intensive research into Japanese art, and the updated Bibliography shows that Hokusai above all has been, as he was from the earliest days of western interest, a constant focus of attention. It follows that inaccuracies and omissions have inevitably come to light, but in essence my view of Hokusai and his art remains unchanged, and to have recast the text would have been to lose its period flavour, written as it was just as the vogue for the Japanese print was beginning, after a long eclipse.

One other survival from that pioneer period of rediscovery is an obsolete form of romanization of Japanese words (e.g. the spellings *ye* for *e* and *gwa* for *ga*). For consistency's sake this earlier form has been retained where Japanese titles have been romanized for the much augmented Bibliography, but books published under titles utilizing the present-day form have, of course, been listed verbatim.

The 'List of Books Illustrated by Hokusai' given in the first edition was perforce drawn up from inadequate sources. As a revised and augmented list will form part of the separate book I have compiled entitled *The Art of Hokusai in Book Illustration*, the obsolete list has been omitted from this edition.

J.H.

The title page of Hokusai's instructional book
Yehon Saishiki Tsū, 1848. *(See page 107.)*

INTRODUCTION

'The delight of studying Hokusai is that
he is such a vast world in himself.'

Fenollosa

THE history of western appreciation of the pictorial art of Japan can be studied in all its phases in relation to the work of one man, Hokusai: first, unreasoning veneration for the new and exotic; next, a reaction and revaluation as knowledge grew and comparison was made with classic western art; and lastly, fresh admiration as we came to understand the intuitive expression in Japanese art of tenets that modern European art has evolved so laboriously. At the first discovery of Japan as a new-found land of painting in the latter half of the nineteenth century, the pioneers became the devotees of what amounted to a cult, in which the worship of Hokusai, as the greatest of the Japanese masters, was one of the first ordinances. Despite the warnings of one or two high-priests of the cult, like Anderson and Fenollosa, to whom, with their better knowledge than most of the works of the great classic masters of the past, such worship was excessive, if not misplaced, there was generally an uncritical and indiscriminate acceptance of the vast, and correspondingly uneven, output of an artist prolific even by Japanese standards.

To us today, he seems to have been praised for the wrong things: for his realism, or for his immense industry, or for his encyclopaedic record of the Japan of his day. De Goncourt even called him the 'true creator of Ukiyo-ye,[1] the founder of the Popular School', whereas, in fact, he came at the very end of a long line of Ukiyo-ye artists, and in his latest works at

least, was scarcely classifiable as Ukiyo-ye at all. He was blamed, if at all, with equal irrelevance. There were always those few voices that, more in sorrow than anger, and more in echo of the native censure than the result of personal conviction, were raised against his vulgarity, his lack of the noble detachment of the finest Kanō and Chinese painters' work: but usually there was the old confusion between subject and treatment, and even if we agree that his gods lack divinity and his commoners fine sentiments, few would now deny his finest landscapes, the 'Fuji in Clear Weather', the 'Wave', the 'Amida Waterfall', a nobility that is above mere class distinction. Yet even so serious a critic as Revon laid this charge of vulgarity almost entirely on the evidence of that *olla podrida* of sketches, the *Mangwa*, and left the 'Thirty-six Views of Fuji' completely out of account.

In the first twenty years of this century there was a re-evaluation, based on a wider acquaintance with the colour-prints of artists of all periods. The taste of print-collectors veered more towards the Primitives and the masters that closely followed, like Harunobu, Kiyonaga and Utamaro, all of whom had the quality of exquisiteness that now appealed. Hokusai, outside of his landscape and bird-and-flower prints, was, if not disparaged, at least somewhat condescendingly given a high place. Ficke, typifying the great American collectors of his generation, wrote, of the *Mangwa*, 'There is something vulgar, childish, under-developed in the mental attitude revealed; it seems a coarse greed for all experience, unlighted by the power to judge

[1] The 'Passing World' school of painters of gay and low life.

and reject, or by any consciousness of the ranks and hierarchies.'

But the period which has seen the growth of an interest in Japanese paintings and colour-prints has seen also a gradual revolution in Europe of the fundamental conceptions of art and aesthetics. The bases of western admiration for Hokusai have shifted ground. The realism, the virtuosity, the fecundity, that so staggered our forbears, awaken little response, but neither are we afraid to accept his wholesome vulgarity nor his alien conventions. Indeed, as the sound and fury of successive manifestos of Impressionism, Cubism, Expressionism and the rest have died down, it has been borne in upon us that, by tradition and without the convention of capricious distortion that mars so much of modern European art, Hokusai enjoyed just that freedom from all laws but those of painting itself, practised just that doctrine of *l'art pour l'art* that protagonists of modernism have preached since Cézanne.

But this tradition, this freedom, were common to all Japanese artists. Hokusai was gifted with extraordinary powers of draughtsmanship and design. His colour-prints are impressive even today when the whole art of the world, from the Altamira caves to the latest Mexican wall-painting, is at our fingertips in gallery or reproduction; and more impressive still if we project ourselves back one hundred years and more, and view them in all the *éclat* of their originality against the background of the Japanese art of the time.

Hokusai has thus resumed much of his former stature in the estimation of the west, but for different reasons. Now he is valued for his especial contribution to the colour-print in landscape and bird-and-flower designs, for his faculty for wonderfully telling design with no other means than that of the woodcut-line and flat washes of block-printed colour, for the verve and expressiveness of his drawing, and for his originality as an illustrator.

But there are still two views in which the art of Hokusai can be held: the Japanese, and the western. In the first it is judged by those standards of excellence that have always prevailed in Japan, with their emphasis on a style of brushwork consistent with the highest ideals of calligraphy, the master art, and on a loftiness of conception quite above anything akin to the mere reportage of everday incident; in the second it is assessed as we assess the drawings and etchings of say, Rembrandt, on the accuracy, economy and expressiveness with which they convey the artist's interpretation of the world about us, on the spontaneity with which landscape or figure seen with the eye is projected on to paper, on the pattern of the composition, on those inexpressible overtones that make, for us, a good drawing. There is no question but that among the native *cognoscenti* of Japanese art a painting by Hokusai is given an inferior place, or that one by Rembrandt would be given an even lower; or that, conversely, among the majority of European critics, the finest Sesshū or Motonobu (two of the classic masters of Japanese painting) would not be ranked even with a mediocre Titian or Rubens.

Yet in an account of Hokusai that aims at anything like completeness, we are forced to apply a nice judgement that takes cognizance of both East and West, viewing his work with something akin almost to impartiality: after all, what is accepted with acclaim today may well be rejected tomorrow: it has been truly said that the one certainty in aesthetics is that there are no certainties.

In dealing with his huge output within the covers of one volume, any selection of prints and paintings for reproduction can only represent a tiny fraction of the number available, and the temptation to concentrate exclusively on what we now consider the greatest series of prints, dating from 1820 onwards, has to be resisted. Hokusai's working life as an artist began as early as 1778 and ended only with his death in 1849, and the earlier decades saw the production of a range of prints and illustrations for books diverse enough in style and matter to have been the work of three or four separate artists. Indeed, Hokusai's practice of changing his art-name at intervals of a few years makes it quite feasible to consider the work of Shunrō, Sōri, Kakō, Hokusai, I-Itsu, Manji and so on, as the work of different men, and in an endeavour to break up into manageable dimensions a full life of 89 years, I have adopted the plan of dividing this book into sections, each dealing with a period coinciding with the use of one or more of his principal art-names.

Such a course is justified on other grounds, too. Although we sense 'progress' in Hokusai's art throughout his career, and there is a recognizable line of development, there is also a series of achievements in quite different styles and separate fields. As Shunrō he is the true child of the Katsukawa School, designing actor-prints in the manner of Shunshō but influenced, like every Ukiyo-ye artist of the time, by Kiyonaga; as Sōri he inaugurates the widespread use of *surimono*, and designs them with an unmatchable delicacy and ingenuity; as Hokusai, produces that pictorial 'folly', the *Mangwa*; as I-Itsu, the great landscape and *kwachō* ('bird-and-flower') series; as Manji, the 'Poems Explained by the Nurse'. There is

little connection between these diverse summits: some, we consider, are higher than others. In landscape we detect a gradual accession of new powers, though even here again, the 'Thirty-six Views of Fuji' of 1823–9 are almost in a different genre from, say, 'Both Sides of the Sumida River' of about 1804.

The one connecting strand is the personality of the artist which does not change in essentials whatever name he appears under, and informs paintings, drawings, prints and book illustrations of the utmost diversity of style with a certain individuality more characteristic than any signature. Sufficient letters and anecdotes have survived, even if his prefaces to books and his art itself were not enough, to prove that Hokusai was one of the most eccentric of men, dedicated to his art with the passion and single-mindedness of a saint to his religion (only his contemporary Turner comes to mind as a rival in this respect) and outside his art having his own standards of conduct which were often at variance with the conventions and customs of his time: a character that was summed up tersely on his tomb in the Sekiōji in his native town: 'renowned original, sincere man'.

CHAPTER ONE

THE UPBRINGING OF AN UKIYO-YE ARTIST

1760-1795

IN Europe, the social standing of the family from which an artist springs is not a decisive factor in determining the height to which he may climb as an artist, however much his earlier efforts may be advanced or retarded by his parents' position. Aristocrat and commoner, Court painter and painter of low-life, are alike considered to have achieved greatness, Rembrandt as much as Velazquez, Turner as much as Cézanne.

But in Japan under the Tokugawa Shōgunate, a period which began at the turn of the sixteenth century and ended only with the revolution in 1868, the reverse was the case. Before this, indeed, in Japan the art of painting was practically confined to members of the nobility itself, and when occasionally those of lower social standing were apprenticed to painters, the only academies open to them were those of the Kanō, Tosa or Chinese Schools, where those styles of painting were inculcated that had been perfected by, and had the approbation of, the aristocracy. With the coming into being of the Ukiyo-ye School, founded soon after the Tokugawa period had commenced and catering, after its aristocratic founder's death,[1] for the lower orders of Yedo society—a school whose style of painting was condemned for its vulgarity by all those exponents and supporters of the methods of the older schools—it naturally came about that would-be painters of humble birth were invariably enrolled as pupils to one or other of the Ukiyo-ye masters, and only exceptionally aspired to the style of their betters. As a practitioner of this Popular style, an artist could never hope to be held in anything more than relatively low esteem by native connoisseurs, and thus even Harunobu, Kiyonaga and Utamaro, to name three Ukiyo-ye masters acclaimed by the west, have never risen to any high place in Japanese estimation. And so it has been with Hokusai.

According to the most likely account, he was born of an artisan named Nakajima Ise, who lived in Honjō, one of the shabbier districts of Yedo (now renamed Tōkyō). Such an artisan was not, by any means, the lowest in the social scale, and the mere fact that he followed a trade which entailed not only the polishing of metal mirrors but no doubt the chasing and engraving of the designs with which they were embellished, proves him to have had in a certain measure a Japanese trait hyper-developed in his son: that of an innate flair for decoration, for applying apt pattern to any given space.

Although we know more, I suppose, of the events in Hokusai's life[1] than of those of almost any other of the great Japanese artists, that does not mean that his life is documented to a degree comparable to that usual in the case of a European painter of equal eminence of the same period. Concerning long periods of his life there is more or less complete silence. Even the reliability of the accounts of his parentage is questionable, as, according to

---

[1]Although Matahei, of Samurai stock, has usually been credited with the founding of the Ukiyo-ye School, he was never a popular painter, and in fact Japanese authorities do not now consider him as the founder. The style was first addressed to the wider, humbler public in the book illustrations of Moronobu and his contemporaries.

---

[1]The chief sources for the events of Hokusai's life are given in the bibliography.

one view, not altogether unsubstantiated, his true father was one Kawamura Ichiroyemon, and he was only the adopted child of Nakajima Ise. An adoption of this sort was quite a common practice when an artist or artisan lacked a son to train as a pupil, and many instances are recorded in the biographies of the Ukiyo-ye artists. Nakajima's wife was believed to be descended from one of the minor figures in that most dramatized of all incidents in Japan's history known to us now under the name of the Chūshingura or 'Loyal League',[1] but whatever blue-blood may have run in her grandparent's veins, her marriage with a humble artisan like Nakajima proves that the colour must have been much attenuated in hers.

Against the adoption theory is the fact that Hokusai must have had brothers, since at a quite tender age he was put out to work in a bookseller's shop, whereas, had he been an only child, he would have been expected to follow his father's, or adopted father's, profession. At this time he was known as Tokitarō. Soon, under the name of Tetsuzō, he was apprenticed to a wood-engraver and went to live in another part of Honjō. From about 1774 to 1777 he plied the craft that in after years was to serve him so faithfully, but although during this period he must have arrived at an understanding of the technical difficulties involved in the engraving process, this knowledge seems never to have led him to simplify his own designs, which often strained the resources of the engraver to the utmost. Wood-engraving was no more an art in its own right in the Japan of Hokusai's day than it was in the Germany of Dürer's: the engraver's task was to make a facsimile of the drawing or writing provided, and it never entered the artist's or calligraphist's head to simplify for the benefit of the engraver.

But it can hardly be doubted that, handling the books in the shop and then engraving the blocks from which they were printed, he was led to try his own hand at designing. During the years as an engraver he had ample opportunities to study the art of illustration, and at eighteen, having probably shown some promise with the brush, he was accepted as a pupil by Katsukawa Shunshō, one of the greatest of the Ukiyo-ye artists, who was then at the height of his powers.

It is interesting at this stage to glance at the state of the Ukiyo-ye school of painting in the year 1777, when Hokusai became one of its recruits. As has been mentioned, its inception in the seventeenth century is usually ascribed to a genius named Matahei, who not only evolved a novel style of painting, borrowing elements from both the Tosa and Kanō (the classical schools), but employed it to record the gay and fashionable world of Yedo, the *samurai* and their courtesans, and also the common folk going about their daily business and pleasure. The soubriquet such painting earned—the words 'Ukiyo-ye' mean literally 'Pictures of the Fleeting World' and figuratively 'Pictures of Gay Life'—gives an inkling of the disapprobation such a descent into the crowded streets, such jostling with the vulgar herd, gave rise to, though the prime fault of the style lay more in the revolutionary manner of painting, the refusal to bow to the dictates of the styles of brushwork that had prevailed for centuries.

Later in the seventeenth century, followers of Matahei like Moronobu and his contemporaries found a new vehicle for their art: book illustration. Reforms of the Tokugawa Shōgunate led to wider education, and the people of Yedo, which was already a populous town, had to be supplied with an ever-increasing flow of literature, a large proportion of which, tales, history, legend, poetry, whether educational or simply entertaining, was illustrated. Apart from the enormous impetus thus given to the designing of illustrations, a demand grew for separately printed sheets that could be hung up for display, like the gentry's *kakemono*, or pasted to screens. These broadsheets were the forerunners of the colour-

---

[1] The Chūshingura is dealt with in Chapter III.

prints of the next century, for passing through stages when they were printed in black outline only and then hand-coloured, about 1740, additional blocks were used to apply colours, limited at first to two only. In 1765 the potentialities of full polychrome printing seem first to have been realized, and after that date up to as many as twelve blocks might be employed to produce a single colour-print. It is generally conceded that technically the work of the engravers and colour-printers reproducing the designs of the Ukiyo-ye artists (and occasionally, of artists belonging to other Japanese schools) has never been approached elsewhere in the world. A succession of great designers arose to make the fullest use of this exquisite medium and Shunshō, the artist under whom Hokusai was now put to study, was one of the most outstanding.

Born in 1726, Shunshō had begun design-ing for colour-prints whilst Harunobu was still alive[1] and by 1777 was one of the acknowledged leaders of the school, with a wide range that included most forms of the Ukiyo-ye print, but a special predilection for the theatrical print, in which sphere he was supreme.

By 1779, Hokusai had evidently finished his apprenticeship and had been given the art-name (*gwamyō*) of Shunrō, with the right to use it with the art-surname (*geisai*) of Shunshō's school, namely Katsukawa. At least one print is extant that can be ascribed to this earliest period, since it represents an actor in a play known to have been performed in the Nakamura Theatre in Yedo in 1779. But it is more likely that Hokusai had already made his debut before the public as an illustrator of

[1]Harunobu, one of the first to use the full colour-print technique and the greatest single influence upon the Ukiyo-ye painters of his generation, died in 1770.

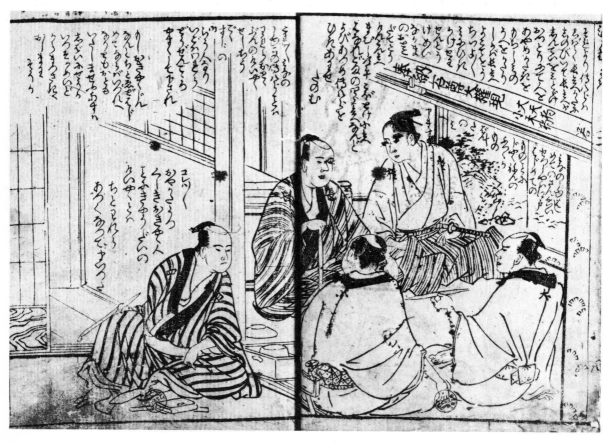

1. Gompachi, the brigand, with companions.
From the kibyōshi Yedo Murasaki, '*The Yedo Violet (or courtesan)*'. *1780.*

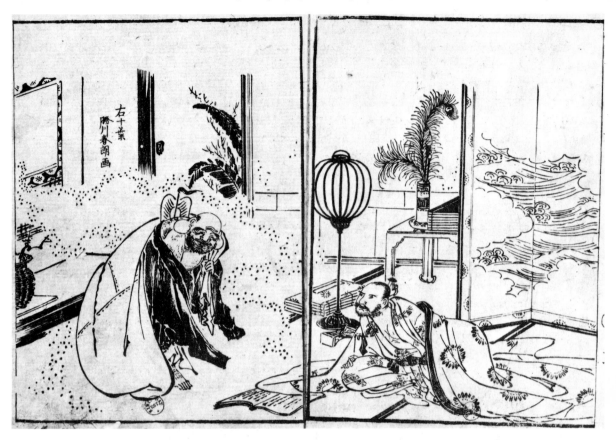

2. The dream of Yōnai, a poor schoolmaster, who bought a painting of Hotei, one of the Gods of Good Luck. The God appears in a dream to teach the schoolmaster how to be successful in life. *From the* kibyōshi Kyōkun Zonagamochi, '*The Chest containing various teachings*'. *1784.*

the little books such as *kibyōshi* (meaning 'yellow-backs', the word having precisely the same meaning and for the same causes, as it has with us and the French), flimsy publications that have in many cases, we may be sure, disappeared without trace. About 1780 he was, as an illustrator of the 'Story of Gompachi and Murasaki', (Fig. 1) one of these *kibyōshi*, still using his earlier name of Tokitarō. For several years, too, he also wrote the text of these trifles, though it should not be assumed that they show any particular literary merit: those most competent to judge in Japan dismiss them as of no account. On the other hand they are evidence that Hokusai, from the age of twenty, had mastered his mother tongue sufficiently well to be able to set down a readable story, a fact that

gives a hint of a study of literature from an early age, and would help to account for the astonishingly encyclopaedic knowledge of Japanese history, legend and custom that his vast output evinces. If we are amazed at the familiarity Shakespeare shows with classical literature, the events of history, the customs and practices of all trades and professions, we shall at least show equal astonishment at Hokusai's immense erudition in the ways of the streets, the habits and lore of *his* people, the associations, legendary and real, of every hamlet, peak and streamlet of his native country.

The earliest works of a great artist are always the object of curiosity, the more so when, as in Hokusai's case, they are separated from his last works by a span of over seventy

3. KATSUKAWA SHUNSHŌ. The actor Matsumoto Koshirō IV in the part of a *samurai. About 1780.*
(*Compare with the work of Shunrō, his pupil, Figs. 4 and 5.*)

4. Women were not allowed to act on the Japanese stage, and certain actors excelled in female impersonation,
like Segawa Kikujirō shown in this print. *Signed Shunrō. About 1784.*

years—he died, brush in hand, when he was eighty-nine.[1] In that immensely long period of activity, during which fundamental develop-

ments took place in the Ukiyo-ye world, the character of the *nishiki-ye,* the 'brocade-print' as the colour-print was called, underwent considerable changes. In regard to technique and style, it is hardly surprising that the young man using the name of Shunrō might well be a different man from Hokusai as we generally think of him, the artist of the

[1]It should be noted that the Japanese account a man already one year old at his birth: hence by Japanese reckoning Hokusai was 90 at his death. This adjustment has to be made when translating Hokusai's age in books or on paintings.

'Thirty-six Views of Fuji', the 'Waterfalls', the 'Imagery of the Poets': there is nothing in common between the two. But Shunrō is much more typically an Ukiyo-ye artist than Hokusai was to be under any subsequent name.

Many of the prints designed by Hokusai up to about 1790 are of actors in character, (Fig. 4) and clearly influenced by Shunshō. By the time Hokusai joined his school, Shunshō had evolved what almost amounted to a formula for recording each stage performance as it was given. Almost invariably, he prepared a series of prints in the narrow upright format (called *hoso-ye*, 'narrow picture') each representing one of the principal actors in the part he played (Fig. 3). More rarely, two such sheets might be joined to form a diptych, and only very exceptionally was the normal sheet, about fifteen inches by ten, employed. Despite the large numbers of such prints extant, with no more, often, than a single figure as subject, the handling of this figure, the arabesque it makes against the lightly-suggested scene of the play, is varied with such skill that monotony would be the last charge one would make against them. A number of prints exist, in this same format and with similar restricted subject-matter, under the signature of Shunrō, and although some of them strike us as rather tame beside the often strikingly dramatic conceptions of Shunshō, there are a few which show signs that Hokusai was an apt pupil who would no doubt have upheld worthily the standards of the Katsukawa School had he been content to remain a follower. The print of Danjurō V, an actor who was all the rage in Yedo at the time, is a fine example of Shunrō's theatrical prints (Fig. 5).

But Shunshō was only one of a number of powerful artists who were working in the early eighties of the century. By 1782 Kiyonaga (1752–1815) was emerging, after a not particularly distinguished debut, as the most potent force in Ukiyo-ye since Harunobu, especially in that other kind of colour-print

5. The actor Danjurō in the play of Toba no Koizuka. *Part of a diptych. Signed Shunrō.*

which rivalled the theatrical in popularity, the kind that recorded the pleasures and fashions of the 'fast set' of the lower classes of Yedo, and especially of the world of the Yoshiwara (the prostitute quarter), the teahouse and other places of amusement and refreshment. For a time both Kitao Shigemasa (1739–1819) and his brilliant pupil Kitao Masanobu (1761–1816) rivalled Kiyonaga as designers of *bijin-ye* ('beautiful-

6. Torii Kiyonaga: The actor Nakazō in private life.
Signed Kiyonaga. About 1783.
(*Figs. 7, 8 and 9 show signs of the influence of this great artist.*)

his types if they were to win favour with the public (Fig. 6). Hokusai, no less than his slightly older contemporary Utamaro (born seven years before Hokusai), succumbed to so pervading and persuasive an influence, and a number of prints exist that, like everything from this halcyon period, are full of the charm of a far-away world peopled by exquisitely clothed girls of gracious mien, with nothing more serious on their minds than the set of their hair, or the knot of their brocade sashes.

One print, of about 1782–3 is of especial interest (Fig. 7). It shows four courtesans of the House called Chōjiya, and from the title of the print, 'Late Spring Designs', was evidently intended to show to the best advantage the fashionably-patterned silks they are wearing. At least three copies of this print are known, and of that number one (in the British Museum) is signed Shunshō, with the 'jar' seal

woman-pictures'), but Shigemasa early turned aside from broadsheet designing and gave himself up largely to book illustration, whilst Masanobu forsook the art almost entirely to devote his energies to novel-writing, in which capacity he appears later in this book as the collaborator with Hokusai in a number of illustrated romances.

Kiyonaga achieved that most signal success of any Ukiyo-ye artist of evolving a new feminine type. Nothing stamped an Ukiyo-ye artist with the seal of greatness so surely as that: it was the mark of Harunobu and of Utamaro, two others of outstanding popularity. Kiyonaga's tall, lissom girl is a singularly sweet and complaisant type, with form and carriage that invite to pleasure. The Yedo menfolk were evidently taken by storm, and Kiyonaga was certainly the most popular and dominant artist of the decade, few artists being able to avoid a near approximation to

7. Four courtesans of the House of Chōjiya.
Sealed Shunrō. (The signature of Kitao Shigemasa is false.)

8. Young boys bringing offerings to Seiōbō, the Fairy Queen of Chinese legend.
One sheet of a triptych. Signed Shunrō. About 1788.

9. Two lovers reconciled by an *Otokodate*. *From a set of*
'*Eight Views of Otokodate'. Signed Shunrō. About 1786.*
(*See below for an explanation.*)

habitually used by him at one stage in his career; another (in the Wadsworth Atheneum) is signed Kitao Shigemasa; and the third is unsigned. All three, however, bear the seal 'Shunrō', the signatures obviously being spurious interpolations aimed to impress western collectors. The style of the print, however, betokens an upbringing in the Katsukawa tradition and a certain leaning towards the Kiyonaga ideal then in its ascendant.

A little later, the surrender to the Kiyonaga influence is even more pronounced. The little print 'Two lovers reconciled by an Otokodate' (Fig. 9) is typical of the prints that were issued in series of six or eight or more, linked under some title, often obscure to us even when translated. The print mentioned, for example, comes from a series entitled 'Eight Views of Otokodate'. The 'Eight Views' had their origin in the traditional classical 'Eight Views of Lake Tung-ting' in China, were trans-

ported by the Japanese to the shores of their own Lake Biwa, and then, by one of those queer transmogrifications so whimsically made by the Japanese and so baffling to us, became a sort of generic title under which a host of incongruous things were seen from eight viewpoints—elegant boudoirs, Yedo tea-houses, lovers' vows, and, in this case, the activities of the famous Otokodate, that is, members of that fraternity who, in Tokugawa Japan, vowed assistance to all unfortunates, friendless or oppressed, in need of succour. In the print reproduced, the sub-title is 'Denkiji's Clear Weather after Storm' and Denkiji the Otokodate is seen with those whom he has protected from some peril, thus signifying the 'Clear Weather after Storm', one of the traditional Eight Views.

Still later, perhaps from 1790, is a series of 'Festivals of the Green-Houses',[1] one for each month. In this set of prints, issuing from one of the foremost publishing houses of the day, that of Tsutaya Jūsaburō, whilst the debt to earlier artists, particularly Kiyonaga, is discernible, there is a warmth of colour and a naturalism in the suave drawing of the limbs that makes the prints delightful on their own account. In the picture representing the sixth month (Fig. 10), the confab of porters, each with his load of merchandise, is cleverly designed, and the leaning figure of one is splendidly caught.

Another fine print, of Kintoki, seems a direct imitation of Kiyonaga, by whom there are a number of similar designs dealing with the exploits of this infant Hercules of Japanese legend. Kintoki is represented as a lusty lad of red-brick hue, gripping a black bear by the neck with his left hand and an eagle by the tarsus with the right, grimacing in the effort, with that down-drawing of the mouth at one side so commonly affected in theatrical prints by the Torii family of artists of whom Kiyonaga was the leader. This print was

---

[1]The 'Green-Houses' were the brothels.

10. Coolies put down their loads to watch
one of their number dance in the 'Sixth-month Festival'.
*From a set of 'Festivals for the Twelve Months'.
Signed Shunrō. About 1790.*

similar subjects from Utamaro's early period, and it is just possible that Hokusai, ready, throughout his career, to borrow and assimilate elements from any new style that swam into his ken, may have seen and admired the Utamaro prints and set himself to emulate them.

About 1785 there appears to have been a rupture with Shunshō. According to the *Katsushika Hokusai den* it was caused by Hokusai flirting with the Kanō style, Shunshō giving vent to his anger at this seeming apostasy by forbidding Shunrō to use any longer the school appellation of Katsukawa. Another story, vouched for by one who maintained he had had it from Hokusai himself, tells how Shunkō, Shunshō's *alter ego*, so closely did he follow his master's style, coming upon a signboard Shunrō had painted for a picture-dealer, tore it down and told the shopkeeper it was an offence to exhibit such a poor thing. Doubt has been cast on these explanations of a rift with Shunshō because the erstwhile pupil continued to use the name Shunrō until 1796, which he is unlikely to have done in the circumstances. On the other hand, it is worthy of note that in at least two little books of 1786, Shunrō announced a change of name to Gummatei, a change that nevertheless proved short-lived. Despite these doubts, it is clear that Hokusai began to draw slowly away from his old master's teaching, and with that avidity for studying new and untried methods which characterized him throughout his life, no doubt found the conservatism of Shunshō, who was still producing actor-prints of a high order at his death in 1792 differing but slightly in externals from those on which he had built up his reputation fifteen to twenty years before, too great a restraint on his restless nature.

published by Yeijudō, another of the very famous print publishers of Yedo.

One other curious type of production of this period remains to be mentioned, the prints that have Chinese subjects. Among these are the 'Chinese Boys at Play' (in the Boston Museum) and the rare triptych in the Victoria and Albert Museum of 'Seiōbō with attendants receiving offerings from young boys' (Fig. 8). The subjects are not so much Chinese as a species of *chinoiserie* only slightly nearer the original than similar exotic fancies by English artists of the eighteenth century. There are a small number of somewhat

CHAPTER TWO

THE ART OF SURIMONO

1796-1800

NOBODY who has studied Japanese art and letters can have failed to have been puzzled and, at times, exasperated, by the custom that permits a man to change his name at will, and to employ a different name for each activity in which he is engaged. Revon illustrates this faculty for assuming, as it were, a separate identity for each different undertaking, with the story of a Japanese student who presented himself for an oral examination under a different name from that under which he had sat for the written.

As with so many other customs which are superficially identical in Europe and Japan but are, in fact, at bottom quite otherwise, so with the giving of names. With us, a name carries with it the idea of permanence; we are registered under it; it is the identifying tag that in time comes to sum up the lifelong personality. In Japan, it has to keep pace with and express the changeableness of a human being, the boy has one name, the growing man another, another is required when he takes a trade or craft, another when he changes his style, and a last and abiding one is only bestowed upon him when he is dead. It must be admitted that Hokusai showed uncommon licence in this respect, and allowed himself more art-names than any other artist, but even in that fact we can see a reflection of the dynamism and the caprice that led to his frequent changes of style, the varying allegiances, the need to try every side-track rather than to keep to the middle of the road. But for collectors and others interested in the art-history of the period, the changes of name often lead to confusion, which is made worse-confounded by the practice of bestow-

ing discarded art-names on pupils, who thereafter bedevil all attempts accurately to identify and classify the master's works. On three occasions in his life at least, Hokusai passed on outlived names, in 1799, Sōri, in 1800, Shinsai, and at some unknown date but about 1820, Taitō, and prints under each signature have become the centre of minor controversy as to which are Hokusai's, which the pupils'.

Some of Hokusai's changes of name are so short-lived and so insignificant in relation to his work that they can be passed over. About 1796, however, a name appears that registers a fundamental change of direction in Hokusai's art: Hyakurin Sōri.

Not a great deal is known of Hokusai's life in the ten years that followed the supposed break with Shunshō. Several references occur in the old biographies to his straitened circumstances, and as a struggling and as yet far from popular designer of broadsheets and illustrations to cheap booklets, it is no surprise to learn that he was obliged to resort to hawking red pepper and calendars in the streets to make ends meet. There would, after all, have been no great descent in the social scale; as a minor artist in his school he was accounted no more than a tradesman, and there are many instances of men who left shop-counter or work-bench to take up print-designing, and also of those who gave up designing to resume mercantile occupations. Kiyonaga, at the height of his fame, turned his back on prints and chose to run a tobacconist's shop; Hokkei, one of the most brilliant of Hokusai's pupils, gave up his fishmongering to become an artist. All the same, Hokusai's pride was such that we can well believe the story that, seeing Shunshō approaching him one day when crying his wares in the street, he turned aside into the crowd to avoid an encounter.

The need to supplement his income from other sources could not have lasted long or interfered much with his main occupation. By 1794 he had sufficiently established himself as a painter to be included as one of a party, of which the renowned painter Kanō Yūsen was also a member, selected to assist in restoration work at the temple of Nikkō. Once again his independence of mind, which led him to criticize a drawing of Yūsen's, brought about a breakdown in relations (Yūsen himself, by other accounts, was a fiery individual and actually committed *harakiri* some years later after a nobleman had spoken slightingly of one of his paintings). Hokusai was debarred from any further part in the project, and the incident may have put an end to any idea he may have had of seceding to the Kanō school.

In taking the name Hyakurin Sōri, Hokusai was merely following the practice of a pupil adopting a name formerly used by his master. How long Hokusai had been influenced by the work of Hyakurin Sōri III (Hokusai was the fourth to bear the name) it is impossible to say, though Revon, no doubt relying on native sources, puts his first leanings in that direction as early as 1787. Although this seems too early, it is just conceivable that it was association with this artist, rather than a Kanō, that aroused Shunshō's disapproval.

Yet it seems unlikely that Hokusai actually took lessons from Sōri, who was active about 1750 to 1780. More probably he studied his paintings and sketches, a number of which may have been in the hands of friends and pupils, and also his illustrations to a book entitled *Segen shūi* 'A collection of proverbs of the world', that had appeared in 1758. Little, apart from his works, is known of Sōri III. His paintings show an indebtedness to two earlier great artists, Tawaraya Sōtatsu (active in the first half of the seventeenth century) and

Ogata Kōrin (1660–1716) and, sealed with a large round seal similar to Kōrin's, have been mistaken for that artist's work. Through him, Hokusai learned something of a style of painting that is perhaps the most Japanese of the Japanese, the furthest from occidental practice and understanding. Kōrin exemplifies in its perfection the Japanese art of decoration, a certain bland adaptation of natural forms—it would be wrong to call it distortion; a subtle play of whimsical imagination, especially in bringing into harmony things oddly incompatible in nature; a power of evocative drawing and composition, sufficiently eccentric to appear the result of a divine intoxication in the artist. Gonse, one of the first to appreciate Kōrin's style, wrote of it,[1] 'Sous des apparences souvent enfantines, on découvre une science merveilleuse de la forme, une sûreté de synthèse que personne n'a possedée au même degré dans l'art japonais et qui est essentiellement favorable aux combinaisons de l'art décoratif.' The artist whose name Hokusai now took had, in lesser degree than Kōrin but still predominantly, a flair for design conceived with fantasy, for treatment that, whilst showing a mastery in the depiction of natural forms, sacrificed everything to compositional effect. These traits occur in greater or less degree in Hokusai's work throughout the rest of his life. They become part of that amalgam of styles that underlies the greatest triumphs of later years: the finest *surimono*, the *Shashin gwafu*, the 'Thirty-six Views', the 'Waterfalls', the 'One-hundred Views of Fuji' and many others.

The little book heralding so much is, it must be admitted, only a playful trifle. The title is rather hesitatingly translated 'Foreigners imitating Japanese customs' and most of the pages show fantastic 'foreigners' engaged in typically Japanese pursuits—negroes exchange New Year's Cards, pygmies try their hands at the 'first writing of the New Year', men from the 'Land-of-the-Pierced-Bodies'

---

[1] *L'Art Japonais*, 1883.

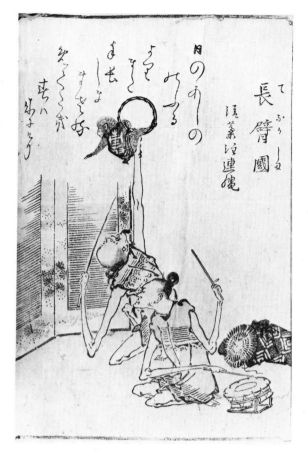 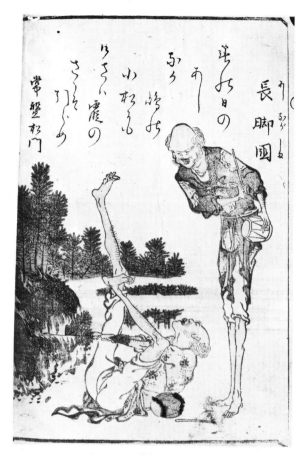

11. The performing monkey was a common sight in Japan and as an illustration to *Shiki Nami-gusa*, a book showing foreigners imitating Japanese customs, 1796, Hokusai shows men from the 'Land-of-the-Long-armed' as monkey-trainer and assistant.
12. Men from the 'Land-of-the-Long-legged' pulling up a young pine tree. Another illustration to *Shiki Nami-gusa*.

fly kites, and, in the illustration shown, men from the 'Land-of-the-Long-armed' act the parts of the monkey trainer and his assistants (Figs. 11–12).

This book (published in 1796), and the adoption of the new name, coincided with a new activity: the designing of *surimono*. As an essentially Japanese form of art and one in whose development Hokusai took a prominent position, it may not be out of place to mention its genesis. As a generic name, *surimono* simply means 'rubbed thing', 'impression', and could be applied to any print, but it came to signify specifically a certain type of usually small print bearing invitation, announcement, or greetings, accompanied as a rule by light verse and decorated with block-printed designs. Although the *surimono* did not

receive its definitive form until Hokusai, prints with a similar purpose had appeared much earlier. In 1765 and the following year, at the very inception of the full colour-printing process, picture calendars (*ye-goyomi*) were exchanged between friends, especially fellow-members of poetry clubs, who often designed their own cards or engaged professional artists like Harunobu or Shōshōken, to whom they supplied the 'idea' on which the picture was to be based, to design them for them. These calendars gave, often in cryptic or ingeniously hidden form, the long and short months of the year, information essential in Japan, under whose calendric system the number of days in each month varies from year to year.

Hokusai seems to have been the first to put

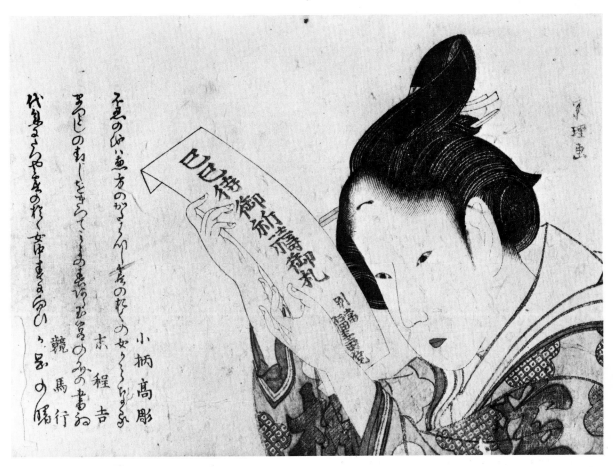

13. A charm from the Shrine of Benten. *A surimono. Signed Sōri. 1797.*

the privately printed 'social-card' to wider use, and as early as 1793, under the signature of Mugura Shunrō, designed one for the musician Tokiwadzu Mojidayu, who announced the adoption of a new name at a concert to be given by his pupils at a place near the Ryōgoku Bridge in Yedo. From that time on, and especially after 1796, Hokusai designed a great number of *surimono,* using first the signature Hyakurin Sōri (sometimes adding the name Hishikawa in tribute to the early Ukiyo-ye master Hishikawa Moronobu) and later, perhaps from 1797, Sōri in conjunction with Hokusai, which latter name then appears for the first time.

From a collection of these *surimono,* one can run the gamut of the social occasions of the Japan of Hokusai's day. There are invitations to little functions, such as poetry readings or

musical entertainments; notifications of all those events needing ceremonial commemoration, such as births, marriages, retirements, changes of name; announcements and advertisements of tea-houses and other places of refreshment and amusement. But chiefly they served simply as New Year's Cards, and as such convey good wishes and auguries for good luck and longevity. For example, in the one entitled 'A Charm from the Shrine of Benten' (Fig. 13), the verselet reads 'In the Year of the Snake it is lucky to turn to the Shinobazu Lake, where is shrined a goddess deep in mist', and this type of riddle-me-ree is counterpart to the pictorial charades that Hokusai often indulged in when designing his *surimono.* In Japan, each year has its zodiacal sign, each bearing the name of one of twelve creatures, and in this print there is also reference to the points of the compass for which the same twelve signs also do service. It was a superstition that in the Year of the Snake it was lucky to turn to that point of the compass represented by the Snake, and the girl depicted is bringing a charm from Benten's shrine lying in that direction. The year in this case was 1797, and the print, trifle though it is, gives some notion of Hokusai's manner at the time.

It will be evident from this specimen that properly to explain the manifold allusions and innuendoes of these prints would call for a book in itself, and the complete art of the *surimono*, consisting as it does in the marriage of the text and design in an intricately veiled message, is bound to elude us. The frequent introduction of the zodiacal year-emblem is of great assistance in dating these prints.[1] Usually they were of small size, not much larger than a playing card, but occasionally the 'long *surimono*' was employed with the happiest results, the sheet being folded in two with the design on one strip and the text on the other (Figs. 14–16). Naturally, the Seven Gods of Good Fortune (Fig. 19), the Emblems of Longevity—Crane, Turtle and Pine—and the Three Lucky Things—Egg-plant, Falcon and Fuji—are favourite subjects, but Hokusai shows the utmost variety and ingenuity, and, on the miniature scale allowed by the print, often achieves an astonishing delicacy.

The *surimono* differed from the broadsheet in that it was invariably a private publication and not sold in the print shops. The number printed was probably far fewer than the usual edition of a broadsheet and great care was expended in the preparation of the print, the engraving was of the most exact, the printing of a most refined kind, helped out often with the use of metal dusts, applied brass and silver and even mother of pearl, and by papers that were chosen for an especially velvety surface. *Surimono* are to the colour-printing art what *netsuke* are to sculpture; there is the same fusion of craftsmanship working with precious materials on a miniature scale, the same intent to surprise by the ingenuity in the choice of subject and the playfulness of the treatment. The *surimono* art is, consequently, rather a 'mixed' art, and viewed simply from the pictorial standpoint is often no more than 'quaint', but seen as a whole, with its express intent in mind, it cannot fail to impress us as something highly civilized and sophisticated.

Many of the *surimono* were designed for members of poetry clubs (Fig. 19), and during these years Hokusai seems to have moved in the circle of the *literati*, or at least those purveying literature of a light kind, and writers of comic novels, like Kyōden, and the composers of the *kyōka*, the humorous verselets so often accompanying the *surimono*. Hokusai's work appears, too, in a number of albums of poetry directed, it would seem, to the more refined among his audience, books produced with unusual care, fine chirography being interspersed with prints that are characterized by the use of gradation-printing in pale colours. In such albums, of which *Yanagi-no-Ito* ('Willow-silk'), 1797, *Otoka-doka* ('The Stamping-dance'), 1798, *Shunkyō* ('Amusements of Spring-time') and *Haru-no Fuji* ('Fuji in Spring'), 1803 (Fig. 20), are typical, the characteristics of the *surimono* are broadened to meet the different medium of the album, and an interesting opportunity is provided of comparing Hokusai's work with that of such long-established artists as Shigemasa and Yeishi,[1] both of whom were also among the contributors to the first two albums named.

This association with the senior artists of the Ukiyo-ye school on an equal footing indicates Hokusai's growing reputation, and

---

[1] Not precisely, as the same sign appears every twelfth year, but other evidence in the print usually helps to pin-point the year.

[1] 1756–1829. Yeishi came of Samurai stock, and all his prints have a refinement that suggests an aristocratic nature.

14. A ferry boat with passengers bearing New Year gifts. *Signed Hokusai Sōri. About 1798.*

15. The Lover's Flute: The famous medieval hero, Yoshitsune, a noted flute player, serenading Princess Jōruri. A 'long surimono'. *Signed Gwakyōjin Hokusai. About 1802.*

16. Chanters of *naga-uta* (dramatic recitations) rehearsing, members of the orchestra trying their instruments. A 'long surimono'. *Signed Gwakyōjin Hokusai. About 1802.*

若水汲子

筆埋光より
又して見れば
うら炎を冬の
あと溶ら名栗
青苔生尤住
被屋の日
をるは
又る様に
く吟ハ
く庭漢す

荒駒早則

雪豊棧
かをさ小ろい
ざ塙り
野なり
は佛
さ耳ころり
な

又百が小ら神
歴陵のけさよ
からかすみの
ろろしきさ紀

17. On the balcony. *A page from* Miyako-dori, *'The Bird of the Capital'. 1802.*

18. A *daimyō's* retainers crossing a bridge. *The first plate in Yeishi's 'Brocade Prints of the Thirty-six Poetesses'.*
Signed Gwakyōjin Hokusai. 1801.

19. Comic poets mimicking the Seven Gods of Good Fortune. *Unsigned. About 1800.*

20. Girls gathering herbs of early spring. *From the album* Haru-no-Fuji, '*Fuji in Spring*'. *1803.*

from 1799 onwards he seems to have had pupils, or at least close followers of his style, who either took names he had discarded, or new art-names based on his own. One Sōji who became Sōri V in 1799, appears to have been the first, Hokuba and Hokujū followed soon after, and Shinsai took a name that Hokusai had used for a brief period at the end of the century. These are the first of a large number of artists—some fifty have been counted—who, in the years to come, showed allegiance to the master Hokusai.

21. A comic poet, Shiraku Yoshina, as a fishmonger.
From 'Fifty Fanciful Poets, each with one poem'. 1802.

CHAPTER THREE

CHŪSHINGURA AND ILLUSTRATIONS TO THE KYŌKA POETS

1798-1806

DURING the years from 1798 to 1806, Hokusai was emerging as one of the most dominant personalities in the Ukiyo-ye school. By the late nineties, as we have already seen, he was contributing to the *kyōka* albums on equal terms with such veterans as Shigemasa and Yeishi and had begun to attract pupils. About this time he showed the greatest vacillation regarding his art-name, and Sōri, Kakō, Hokusai, Gwakyōjin Hokusai, Hokusai Shinsei and Shinsai were all used, some of them concurrently. The continued study of opposing styles of painting in Japan and a growing interest in those of China and even of Europe provided conflicting influences that resulted in changes in Hokusai's own style.

There are some exceedingly interesting prints in the orthodox Ukiyo-ye tradition of 'loving couples' or *bijin-ye* ('beautiful women') under the signature of Kakō.[1] Some, like the one illustrated (Plate III), seem to show a lingering on of the Kiyonaga tradition with something added that makes it, and one or two others of the same series,[2] quite unlike anything else being produced at the time, though perhaps they are nearest to certain prints of Utamaro. Utamaro had by this time taken the place of Kiyonaga as the leader of the Ukiyo-ye school, and now it was his tall, languorous courtesans who were fashionable with the Yedo print-buyers. Indeed for some

years now, his only rival had been Toyokuni, head of the Utagawa sub-school, a brilliant artist who designed many fine prints in the earlier part of his career, but whose work went sadly downhill after 1800 when he sought to satisfy the demands of a public with a craze for actor-prints and far less taste and discrimination than their forbears. That Hokusai was acquainted with Toyokuni is proved by their collaboration in a book published in 1804, Toyokuni illustrating the first volume and Hokusai the second, but Toyokuni had apparently little to offer to Hokusai who, in any case, had now ceased to produce theatrical prints. Utamaro, however, whose superb 'Large Heads' and half-length portraits had been appearing in the nineties, could not have failed to stir Hokusai; and in another set of prints, the very title of which, 'Seven Fashionable Bad Habits', is exactly what we might have expected from Utamaro, Hokusai comes even closer to the Utamaro style, though the cast of features, the shape of the head, of Hokusai's girl is unmistakable. In one of the rare prints[1] of this set, a bust-portrait and a half-length of two girls, one is shown cleaning her teeth and is guilty of the 'bad habit' of showing her teeth, the other, talking to her, is showing her tongue, an equally reprehensible failing. Even the quasi-moralizing implicit in the print is reminiscent of Utamaro's tongue-in-cheek sermonizing. But Hokusai may have realized that he stood little chance of competing with so famous a rival in a sphere Utamaro had made his own, and the

---

[1] Toda has shown that the correct reading for the characters hitherto read Kakō is probably Sorubekō, but Kakō has been used so long that it is thought best to retain this reading.

[2] The series was one of famous lovers and besides the 'Azuma and Yogoro' reproduced, prints of 'Date no Yosuke and Seki no Koman' and 'O-Hatsu and Tokubei' are also known.

---

[1] Reproduced in Stewart, *Subjects Portrayed in Japanese Colour-Prints*, 1922.

number of prints of this kind by Hokusai are sadly few.

The signature Kakō is probably best remembered for the first broadsheet series based on the Chūshingura. This, the most famous play of the popular stage, the *kabuki*, was much in Hokusai's mind in these years; at least two comic or parodied versions appearing in 1802 in book form and the two separate, more orthodox broadsheet series about 1798 and 1806.

Any study, however slight, of the Chūshingura, brings us up against a core of traits fundamental to the Japanese character and way of life. The idea of loyalty, of selfless service, was implicit in the smallest unit, the family, as it was in the largest, the state. The respect of the child for the parent was proverbial, the devotion of a *samurai* to his overlord no less unquestionable, the fanaticism in time of war simply the expression of service and obedience to a superior, and thus ultimately to the Emperor, underlying the thought and action of every true Japanese. The historical incident that gave rise to the play was simply an extreme example of loyalty, and those responsible, the Forty-seven Rōnin, have been canonized in the Japanese martyrology for an act of murderous vengeance that in Europe would more likely have earned them eternal opprobrium.

The incident arose through the inflexibility of Court etiquette. Once a year, the *de facto* ruler, the Shōgun in Yedo, received an ambassador from the *de jure* Emperor in Kyōto, and the occasion was attended by much pomp and circumstance. A meticulous observance of the etiquette of the occasion made it necessary for the two officers appointed to receive the Ambassador to undergo a course of instruction from a high court official versed in these recondite matters. In the play[1] Yenya and Wakana no Suke were the two lords deputed to receive the Ambassador, and

Moronao their tutor. Moronao was undoubtedly a most villainous character who adopted a contemptuous attitude towards his charges and could only be propitiated by payment of heavy bribes. The followers of Wakana succeeded in buying their master off from the insults of Moronao, but Yenya was less fortunate, and one day, goaded beyond endurance, he drew his sword with intent to kill his tormentor, but succeeded only in wounding him. The penalty for drawing a weapon in the precincts of the Palace was death, and Yenya, with all the ghastly ceremonial that attended such a function, duly disembowelled himself.

Yenya's retainers, his *samurai*, were thus left without a master and became what was termed *rōnin*, literally 'wave-men', meaning free, wandering, masterless. Some of them, to the number of forty-seven, bound themselves together with a vow to avenge their master's death, hence the title *Chūshingura*, meaning 'Loyal League'. After many frustrating delays, they eventually accomplished their purpose; Moronao, trapped in his surrounded castle, was beheaded by the leader of the Forty-seven Rōnin after refusing an invitation to commit *seppuku*, or suicide by disembowelling.

But the most astonishing act, to us, was yet to follow. The Rōnin had themselves, in destroying Moronao, committed an offence against the laws: unhesitatingly, as a body, they gave themselves up and submitted themselves to the rites of *seppuku*. Their mission was accomplished, honour was satisfied, the penalty was embraced with eagerness.

Although the play credits them with this heroic self-sacrifice, as a matter of historical fact it was far otherwise, for something near a national crisis was precipitated by the condemnation of these men to commit *seppuku*. The Forty-seven Rōnin at once became venerated for their bravery and devotion. The events of the tragedy became matter for dramatization, Chikamatsu, who is some-

---

[1] The historical facts, which differ considerably from the action of the play, are recorded in Murdoch's *History of Japan*, Vol. III.

I. The lover in the snow. *A surimono. Signed* Zen (*previously*) *Sōri Hokusai. About 1798.*

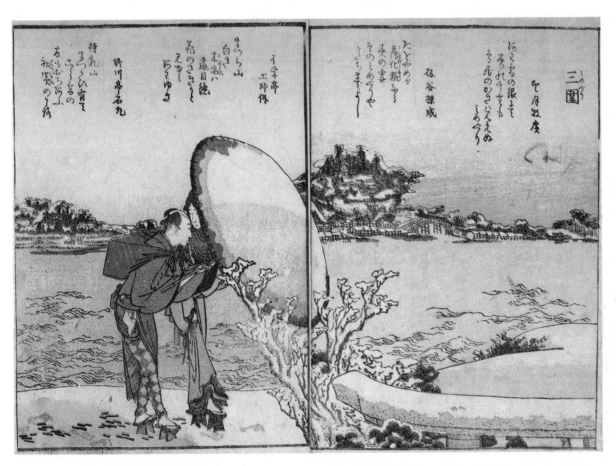

II. Mimigure in the snow. *From 'Fine Views of the Eastern Capital at a Glance'. 1800.*

III. Azuma and Yogorō, two celebrated lovers. *Signed Kakō. About 1798.*

IV. Act V of the *Chūshingura* (1806 version): Sadakuro murdering Yōichibei.
On the umbrella are the words 'New Print, year of the Tiger', i.e. 1806. Unsigned.

22. Act I of the *Chūshingura* (earlier version): Yenya's wife between Moronao and Wakana no Suke.
Signed Kakō. About 1798.

times termed the Japanese Shakespeare, producing a play for the marionette theatre based on the story as early as 1706,[1] a precursor of some forty or fifty others that appeared in the course of time. The definitive play, however, was that of Takeda Idzumo and collaborators, produced first in 1748 and holding its popularity ever since.

It was forbidden during the Tokugawa Shōgunate to use the real names of persons of high rank or to deal with the events of recent history either on the stage or in pictures. Hence the scene of the drama was shifted from Yedo in the eighteenth century to Kamakura in the fourteenth, and the names of the participants in the affair were garbled. Almost every artist of note in the Ukiyo-ye school designed a set of prints based on the drama or portrayed favourite scenes, and

invariably took greater liberties with the dramatists' texts than the dramatists had taken with the historical facts. A book could be written dealing with the variations in, additions to, parodies and burlesques of the traditional eleven scenes, the artists' representations often having only a most tenuous connection with the play, a connection obvious to a literate Japanese familiar with the moves made by the artist in his game of 'Transitions', but often doubtful to us.

Under the signature Kakō, Hokusai's set of prints adheres fairly closely to the story and employs what might be called an *Uki-ye* technique in depicting the scenes. *Uki-ye* were views in which perspective was used in the European manner (or something like it) to give recession in space, a method alien to oriental conceptions and never quite mixing with the more purely Japanese elements of their style, the result being prints that surprise

[1]*Goban Taiheki*, 'The Great Peace'.

23. Act I of the *Chūshingura* (1806 version): Moronao offering a love-poem to Kaoyo.
Seal-dated 1806. Unsigned.

as our own language does when we hear it spoken in broken accents. Earlier artists like Okumura Masanobu[1] and Utagawa Toyoharu[2] had specialized in the *Uki-ye*, usually giving bird's-eye views of places of interest, and Hokusai under the names of Shunrō and Hokusai, produced a few such prints.

The scene reproduced (Fig. 22), the first, in which Moronao is making advances to Kaoyo, the wife of Yenya, is typical. The bands of red cloud, and the descriptive panel to the right of the print, were, like the elaborate perspective, part of the *Uki-ye* convention. The series is hardly a moving one. The figures are too minute to convey any real sense of drama, the buildings too painstakingly drawn to give any impression of grandeur. Even the

trees with their tall leafless trunks are perfunctorily drawn as if with the trees of the Dutch polders, remembered from the third-rate European prints that found their way into Japan, in mind.

It is interesting to compare prints of this series with those of the much more impressive set of 1806. (Two of the prints have the seal-date of that year.) In these prints, the figures are much bolder, the action more significant, and the fragments of landscape viewed beyond the buildings show a new treatment that is not far removed from the masterly handling of the 'Thirty-six Views' of some fifteen years later. Act I is again reproduced for purposes of comparison with the earlier series (Fig. 23). In the other, Act V, 'Murder at Night' (one of the dramatist's interpolations), Hokusai gives a superb rendering of the chaotic darkness covering the fell murder, the boar rushing over the fields being one of

[1] 1686–1764, one of the greatest of the primitives, responsible for a number of innovations in technique.
[2] 1733–1814, founder of the Utagawa sub-school, of which Toyokuni, already mentioned, was in his day the leading light.

those touches that make him so great as an illustrator (Plate IV).

The collaboration of Hokusai with the comic poets has already been mentioned. A number of illustrated poetry books are directly due to this association. The picture book *Adzuma asobi* ('Amusements of the East' [Yedo]), first published in 1799 and consisting largely of open-air views in the capital, might be considered as an evidence thus early of a special interest in landscape, but in fact, the pictures are cast very much in the mould that already existed for this type of semi-guide book. For although the pictures have as their origin the humorous verses of a society of *kyōka* writers and the title is really an old name for a Shintō ceremonial dance accompanied by songs, Hokusai hardly attempts at all to illustrate the poems, but simply gives them a 'local habitation', the book being very much akin to the *meisho-ki* (records of famous places, guide-books), then current, in which bird's-eye views were peopled by humans of ant-like dimensions. In these views, Hokusai is evidently still encumbered by an imperfectly assimilated knowledge of perspective, and the combination of 'lines vanishing at a point on the horizon' with the now anachronistic Tosa convention of long bands of vapour to indicate separation of planes (or simply to avoid tedious detail) is not a happy one. In the colour version of the book, which appeared in 1802, the shortcomings are even plainer.

Hokusai is alleged to have studied the European manner under Shiba Kōkan[1] and the Tosa style under Sumiyoshi Hiroyuki[2] but only, it seems, to graft upon his own already eclectic style such elements as appealed to him in the alien styles of those contemporaries. Sometimes, as in this case, the separate constituents did not knit closely together. In a set of small prints entitled *Oranda Yekagami Yedo Hakkei* ('Eight Views of Yedo Mirrored in the Dutch Style') the debt to European methods is more clearly recognized, but the prints are oddities and were clearly meant to surprise by their very outlandishness.

In *Adzuma asobi*, Hokusai is at his best in the crowd scenes and those where the figures fill the page, among the most successful being the pictures of the doll-shop at Jippendana, the dried-seaweed shop at Tawaramachi, and the tradesmen, stirrup-makers, winders of hair-cords, print-sellers and dyers. The shop of the well-known publisher Tsutaya Jūsaburō is of particular interest, enabling us to stand at the counter, with the well-born *samurai*, turning over the piles of prints fresh from the printers in the back-room, prints of actors in the latest hit at the theatre at Sakaichō, of beauties we flock to see in the Yoshiwara parade. Many have stretched their imagination still further and seen, in the obsequious old bookseller seated at his desk, the publisher to whom print-lovers owe so much, but if it is intended to be Tsutajū, it must have been a memorial portrait only, as the publisher had died in 1797 (Fig. 25).

The *Tōto Shōkei Ichiran* ('Fine Views of the Eastern Capital') of 1800 marks a considerable advance on the *Adzuma asobi*: the warring elements have been brought into greater harmony, the figures are larger and more significant, and the landscape backgrounds are put in with a much surer touch (Plate II). The tints used are bright pinks, mauve, yellow and green, and the effect in a fresh copy is one of springtime gaiety. But throughout it is the figures, rather than the landscapes, that predominate, small dainty figures drawn now in a style peculiar to Hokusai, in no way to be confused with those of, say, Utamaro, whose book of 1801, *Shiki no hana*, 'Flowers (i.e. courtesans) of the Four Seasons' offers an interesting comparison.

Two other, slightly later, books of colour-prints have a kinship with the two already referred to and should be mentioned here, the

---

[1] 1747–1818. Originally a gifted Ukiyo-ye designer, pupil of Harunobu, who later learned the art of copper-engraving and perspective from the Dutch in Nagasaki.
[2] 1755–1811. His most typical work was the painting of Chinese sages on sliding panels in the Imperial Palace at Kyōto.

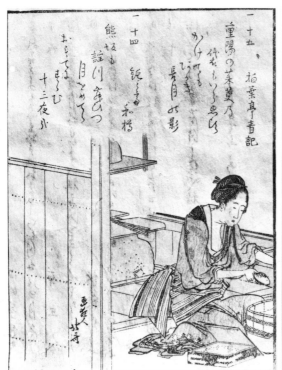

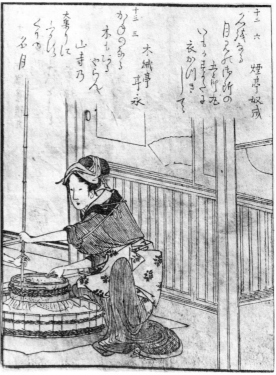

24. Grinding rice. *From the book of 'Comic Poems of the Shishōan Club'. Signed Gwakyōjin Hokusai. About 1798.*

25. The interior of the print and book shop
of Tsutaya Jūsaburō.
From the 'Amusements of the Eastern Capital'. 1799.

Yehon Kyōka Yama Mata Yama[1] ('A picture book of kyōka: Range upon Range of Mountains') and *Yehon Sumidagawa Ryōgan Ichiran* ('Both Banks of the Sumida River at a Glance'), both of which appeared about 1804–5. Hokusai has now completely mastered this species of 'Figures with landscapes' and some of his most charming compositions are the result. There is little or none of the power of synoptic design which is the strength of the later landscape prints, but they represent the culmination of Hokusai's earlier manner, based largely on the earlier Ukiyo-ye masters, combining pleasant features of the *surimono* and the albums, the elegant mincing figures, the pretty colours, the humour. The *Yama mata yama* is a series of separate views of Yedo, each with something of the finesse of the poetry albums.

In the 'Sumida River' book, Hokusai contrives an immense panorama that runs on from page to page, carrying us through

[1]The pictures are all of Yama-no-te, the higher parts of Yedo to north and north-west of the town. Hence the title with its customary exaggeration.

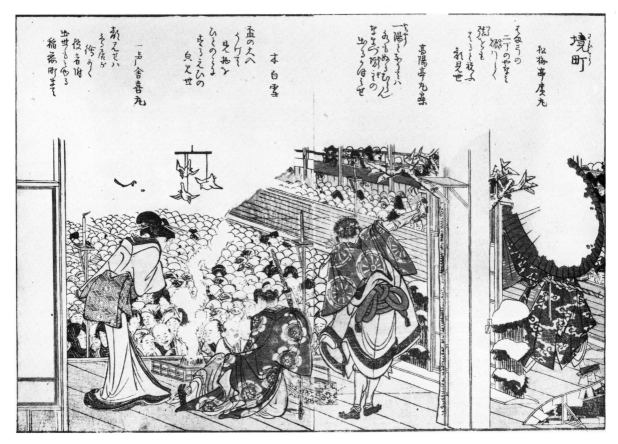

26. Backstage at the theatre at Sakaichō. *From 'Fine Views of the Eastern Capital at a Glance'. 1800.*

morning, noon and night, from New Year's day, through the heats of summer and the autumn rains to the winter snow. It is a tour-de-force of designing in the *makimono* style, which employed a long roll many feet long, a land-leaping transcript that was never looked at as a whole but only piecemeal, a little being unrolled at a time. The drawing is altogether stronger in the three volumes comprising the work than anything of the same kind that Hokusai had so far produced, the designs are more daring, and generally he begins to show signs of the virtuosity, the facility, that later one takes so much for granted (Fig. 28).

Two sets of separately issued prints belonging to the early years of the century are a link between the *surimono* and the type of illustrated book I have been discussing. One is a quarter-block and the other a half-block set of the 'Fifty-three Stations of the Tōkaidō'. This great highway between the old capital, Kyōto, and Yedo, the new, proved a wonderful attraction to the Ukiyo-ye artists, giving them an everlasting scene of activity familiar to their clientèle, passing processions, people on horseback or carried in litters, fording streams or climbing mountain paths, and the fifty-three stations along the route provided just that set runic number so dearly loved by the Japanese artists—the Three Laughers, the Six Jewel Rivers, the Seven Scenes from the life of Komachi, the medieval poetess, the Thirty-six Views of Fuji, the Fifty-three Stations of the Tōkaidō, the Sixty-nine Stations of the Kisokaidō and so on, just as we have the Seven Wonders of the World, the Nine Worthies. The quarter-block series are signed Gwakyōjin[1] Hokusai or simply Hoku-

[1]'The man mad about drawing.'

27. A girl bathing in gold, personifying Prodigality.
From 'The Tactics of General Oven'. 1800.

merchants. The last page gives a portrait of Hokusai with head shaved in the manner customary with artists, poets and priests (Fig. 29). Hokusai's letter accompanying the portrait says 'I am submitting to you my poor fiction. If this can be of any use to you, please publish it after your inspection. As this is my first attempt, please ask the master Kyokutei Bakin to correct my errors, and if this has any success this year, I shall try again next spring, and present the results to you. To Tsutaya Jūsaburō, Tenth day of the Tenth Month.'[1] The reference to Bakin is of note and there is a suspicion of irony in the humble attitude adopted towards the novelist, between whom and Hokusai a stormy association was soon to commence.

About 1804, we hear of the first of those feats of prodigious 'pictorial prestidigitation' that helped to spread Hokusai's fame both as artist and as eccentric. On the occasion of the celebration of one of the festivals at the temple of Gokokuji in Yedo, before a public audience, he drew an immense figure of Daruma, the Buddhist patriarch and saint, using a brush the size of a besom, and great bowls of Chinese ink. So big was the picture—it was roughly 200 yards square—that only by viewing it from the roof-tops could the populace make out what Hokusai had drawn. The prodigy was acclaimed by the mob, and feats of a similar type were performed in other localities. Such performances were dear to the spectacle-loving Japanese and no doubt they helped to increase the popularity of the artist who was probably already a notorious figure, pointed at in the street because of his unkempt appearance and his reputation for eccentric behaviour.

Not long after this public performance, Hokusai had the singular honour, for an Ukiyo-ye artist, of being commanded to

sai and are known to have been issued early in 1804. They were prepared with the same care and on the same miniature scale as *surimono*, which they exactly resembled, even down to the accompanying poems extolling the products for which each place was noted. The other set is perhaps even more interesting for the bold conventionalizing of natural forms of river, hill and tree, and, with a sunny yellow and other fresh tints prevailing, these prints are among the best of the period (Plate VI).

Among the smaller books published about this time, the one entitled *Kamado Shōgun Kanryaku no Maki* ('The Tactics of General Oven') is of interest partly because a change is evident in the style of the drawings compared with earlier *kibyōshi*, the Katsukawa style having now, by 1800, completely disappeared (Fig. 27); and partly because Hokusai was the writer of the book, a humorous work with an impossible plot dealing with the finances of

<hr>

[1]Translated by Kenji Toda in the Ryerson Catalogue. For Bakin see next chapter.

28. A shower at Shin-Yanagi Bridge. *From the picture-book 'Views along Both Banks of the Sumida River'. 1804–5.*

perform in the presence of the Shōgun, Iyenari, and to compete with Shazanrō Bunchō, a very great artist of the Chinese school. It was a contest in which each artist had to make a painting on the spot. It is not recorded what Bunchō drew, but Hokusai evidently gained the day by a trick of showmanship, for, first painting a large paper screen with the great curves of a blue river, he forced a cock, whose feet he had daubed with red paint, to run over it, and described the result as the River Tatsuta in autumn, with the red maple leaves floating down-stream.

In 1806 Utamaro died, and with him, that particular phase of Ukiyo-ye art that had relied so much on exquisitely garbed women for its effect. Utamaro's own standards in his later years had deteriorated, and pupils like

Tsukimaro and Hidemaro, and copyists like Yeizan, succeeded only in developing an altogether coarsened form of *bijin-ye*, so that, just at this time, the hopes of the Ukiyo-ye school were fixed upon Hokusai. He was now unquestionably a master in his own right, the idol of the Yedo crowd, the publishers' star attraction: where before he may have been tentative, held back by remembrance of older styles, experimenting with the new and untried, now there was complete freedom from all restraint, a temptation to spread his wings. Some of the eccentricities of future years, the capriciousness and the buffoonery, the unselective jotting down of everything under the sun, the straining after impossible effects, date from this release from the former bonds, but so also does the growing mastery in

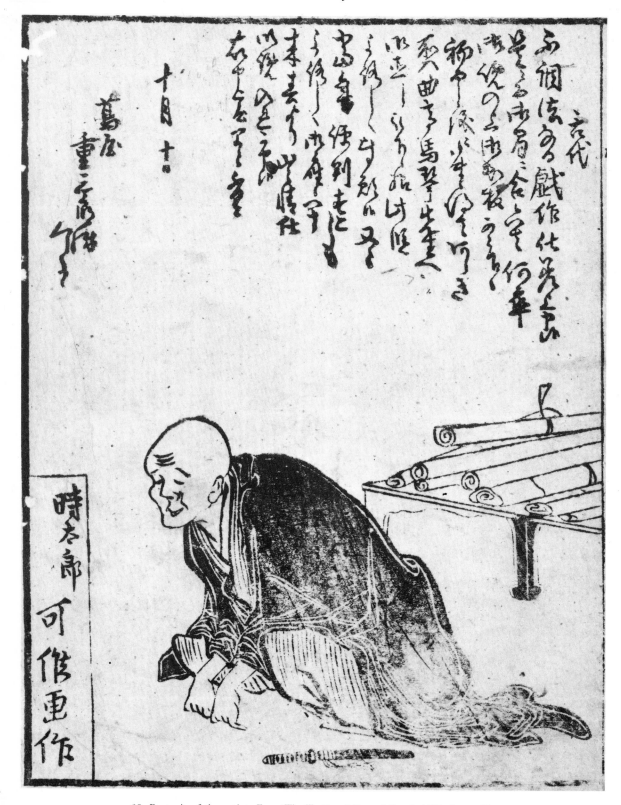

29. Portrait of the artist. *From 'The Tactics of General Oven'. 1800. See p. 40.*

30. Interior of a theatre with a play in progress. *A* uki-ye *or 'perspective' print, about 1794. Signed Shunrō.

landscape and *kwachō*, the amazingly effective draughtsmanship with the brush which becomes, whatever its shortcomings, as expressive as any the world has known. Perhaps it was no coincidence that he began to give himself about this time the school name of Katsushika,[1] a name taken from the district in which he had been born. It was the gesture of a man assured of his place.

---

[1] One of the earliest appearances of this name is on a *surimono* of an old plum tree in bloom, dated 1806.

CHAPTER FOUR

BOOK ILLUSTRATION: THE MANGWA;
SHASHIN GWAFU

1807-1819

FOR the next ten or twelve years by far the greater part of Hokusai's work was in book illustration.

In Japan, from the early seventeenth century onwards, books were illustrated with a frequency that grew steadily with the years, and in addition to 'illustrated books' it became the practice to publish *yehon* or 'picture-books' with little or no text, which represent something especially Japanese and practically without a counterpart anywhere else in the world.

Drawing and writing are much nearer together in Japan than they are in any western country: both require skill in the use of the brush and are looked upon as branches of the same art. It is natural, too, for the Japanese to decorate every article of use, and indeed, in their eyes, the flowing forms of their script are sufficient decoration in themselves. None the less, the flair for ornament often led to an overflow beyond the bounds of the chirography of their written language, and, from early in the seventeenth century, pictures made their appearance as much to embellish the page as to illustrate the written word. Besides this, until comparatively recently, generally there was no printing in our sense of the word, no typography, no type founts,[1] the books being printed by hand from engraved wooden blocks. It was just as easy

for the craftsman to engrave a drawing as the brush-written word. In Europe, medieval 'block-books' such as the *Biblia pauperum* were of this type of printing from blocks on which both text and illustration have been engraved, but here, with the introduction of movable types, the method lapsed.

All these features, kinship of writing and painting, decorative flair, facility of engraving and printing, were conducive to the illustration of books in Japan to a far greater degree than has ever been customary with us: and in respect of the class of books we are considering, the novels and lighter literature of Hokusai's day, there is little doubt that yet another consideration operated, the need to assist the not-quite-literate to an understanding of the novel, poem, play or legend, the need even, going a stage further, to produce books with the minimum of text, books that were a mere collection of drawings completely expressive in themselves.

It can be well imagined that concentration on book illustration affected, if it did not actually form, Hokusai's style. An altogether different technique was called for from that which as a painter pure and simple he might have cultivated, and often, in his paintings, we sense the difficulty the artist has been under of throwing off the restraints of a miniature scale of drawing, of acclimatizing himself to the full-size *kakemono* after being confined to the book-sheet.

The books fall into a number of distinct classes, distinguishable to the Japanese by the colour of the book-covers. Without going into details, we may divide them into booklets, usually of a comic type, of which the yellow

[1]Movable types of wood or bronze were introduced to Japan from Korea about 1595 and Chinese and Japanese classics were sometimes printed in this way, the earliest being those produced by Suminokura So-an (1571–1632), a wealthy dilettante, and Honnami Kōyetsu, a renowned artist and sword expert who flourished in the early years of the seventeenth century. But these are the exceptions to the general rule.

backs (*kibyōshi*) are the commonest; the *yomihon*, larger reading books, mostly novels; books of sketches like the *Mangwa*; poetry books like the *Tōto Shōkei Ichiran* and others described in the previous chapter; and the more lavishly, and often privately, printed albums of poetry.

The *kibyōshi* have already been discussed earlier and a few typical pages reproduced. Such books are rarely of any great artistic consequence. The *yomi-hon*, however, constitute an important part of Hokusai's output as a book illustrator. The literature is of a higher order than that of the *kibyōshi* and prompted a more serious approach on the illustrator's part. In this class are the novels of Bakin (1767–1848), considered by many Japanese as their greatest novelist, and the association between Hokusai and Bakin, almost exact contemporaries, gave rise to some of the most interesting anecdotes of their careers.

The collaboration seems to date from 1807 when both were mature artists and assured of their public. Hokusai was forty-seven, Bakin forty. In this year Hokusai illustrated *Sono no Yuki*,[1] two other novels, and the first part of the book which was to cause a break between the two men, *Shimpen Suiko Gwaden*, Bakin's translation of one of the greatest of Chinese historical novels.

Bakin occupies, or perhaps it would be truer to say, did occupy until recently, a unique place in Japanese literature, without a rival as the most popular novelist the country has ever known. European critics best able to judge have condemned his most famous works as tedious, pedantic, insufferably long and wildly improbable, but unaccountably these characteristics seemed to cast a spell over his Japanese readers—always ready to venerate scholarship, especially in Chinese matters—most of his novels passing through innumerable editions and still being widely

read today, though there is a tendency nowadays to temper the former adulation with a saner criticism, which never, let it be said, assails the place of the novels as classics of Japanese literature.

The relations between Hokusai and Bakin were stormy almost from the start. Both men were of decided individuality, neither given to tolerance of other people's views or feelings. Above all, each was extremely proud and jealous of his art, and it is to this that the quarrels between them are mainly to be attributed, the writer accusing the artist of departing from the text, the artist complaining of the lack of opportunities the text gave him. They were not the first collaborators to fall out, nor the last. Another example, quite near home, was that of Utamaro, the illustrator, and Ikku (d. 1831) the writer, of the 'Annals of the Green-Houses', 1804. With them, as with Bakin and Hokusai, it was the very popularity of the joint work that gave rise to the altercation, the writer and the artist each claiming he was the cause of the book's success. We look at these books for the illustrations primarily, but among the Japanese it was a difficult matter to decide whether text or pictures should be awarded the palm. In the case of the *Shimpen Suiko Gwaden*, the matter came to a judgement, and the publisher, faced after the first ten volumes of Part I with a refusal from Bakin to proceed with the text if Hokusai continued to be the illustrator, and from Hokusai to make further illustrations if Bakin continued to write the text, decided to sacrifice Bakin, another writer named Takai Ranzan bringing to a dull end what Bakin had so brilliantly begun. If one needed any further evidence of the importance given to the illustration of a book in Japan, this incident would provide it: it is impossible to imagine Chapman and Hall discontinuing a novel by Dickens after the first volume because Cruikshank had objected to the text.

These illustrations to the Chinese novel are generally uninspired, but they mark the early

---

[1] For the theme of this and other novels illustrated by Hokusai see de Goncourt's *Hokousai* and the Ryerson Catalogue.

31. Chinese torture. *From volume 9 of 'Illustrated New Edition of* Suikoden'. *1807.*

stages of what has been termed the 'Chinese' element in Hokusai's style. Bakin, in his introductory note to the book above-mentioned, draws attention to illustrations in earlier Chinese editions of the novel, and Hokusai very likely studied such Chinese originals. But too much stress should not be placed on the Chinese character of his drawing; it is some distance from any such originals; no nearer to them, perhaps, than an Italian of the Renaissance was to the Greek models that were his source of inspiration. The women have their hair dressed in the Chinese style, the men have exotic-looking whiskers and are accoutred in outlandish armour, but although they may have passed muster as Chinese, as Rembrandt's biblical figures were accepted as authentic Hebrew, the drawings are very much Hokusai and only superficially Chinese (Fig. 31).

The novels of Bakin and others of the time are invariably based on revenge or jealousy, the mainsprings of most Japanese stories, and are full of murders, suicides, violence in every shape and form, phantoms, transmogrifications and all sorts of supernatural phenomena. Hokusai seizes to the full the dramatic possibilities of the homicidal mania which is the mainspring of the plots, and nearly every volume has fiery designs which certainly do not fall behind the novels in bloodiness and horror. The page from the *Kanadehon Gojitsu no Bunshō*, a sort of sequel to the Chūshingura, is a fair example (Fig. 32), the ghost scene from 'The Story of the Craftsman of Hida' another (Fig. 33).

The books from the year 1806 onwards show a marked development away from the style prevalent in books and prints up to that date, and in nothing is this more evident than

32. An illustration to Yemba's novel *Kanadehon Gojitsu no Bunshō*, a sequel to the *Chūshingura*. *1808*.

33. Priest Funanushi is visited by his daughter's ghost.
An incident from Rokujuen's novel 'The Story of the Craftsman of Hida'. 1808.

34. The cruelties of Dakki, the Concubine of Emperor Chou Hsin. *Signed Hokusai. Diptych. Seal-dated 1807.*

in the drawing of the women. Up to 1806, with 'Both Sides of the Sumida River' as a good example, the slim *musume* forms have been characteristic of the early Hokusai, but still akin to those of Utamaro, Kiyonaga or even Harunobu: now he evolves a far more flesh-and-blood woman, drawn with something nearer to naturalism, and there is a break with the idyllic, fanciful world that he had peopled before.

Separately printed sheets are rare at this period, but the diptych, the 'Cruelties of Dakki the Concubine', 1807, illustrates these developments, the pseudo-Chinese manner, and the taller, more substantial figures: moreover, the stylization in the drawing of human beings, later to develop to such a degree that his men and women seem to

belong to some tribe or race unknown outside the realm of Hokusai, is already evident (Fig. 34).

Other separate prints of note of this time are the series of 'portraits' of the Six Poets.[1] They are yet another instance, of a playful kind no doubt, of the kinship between writing and drawing. By one of those odd caprices which we would no more countenance in serious art than we would a pun in a funeral oration, Hokusai has formed the outline of each of the poets from the brush strokes of the Chinese characters forming the poet's name. This feat of drawing personages with their

---

[1]One of the traditional 'groups' of poets, consisting of Kisen Hōshi, Ōtomo no Kuronushi, Ono no Komachi, Ariwara no Narihira, Sōjō Henjō and Bunya no Yasuhide.

own names was frequently attempted in both Japanese and Chinese art and called for the utmost ingenuity in the adaptation of the brush strokes (and often an extreme elasticity in the forms of the Chinese characters). Hokusai has in this instance employed a technique based on that of the Tosa School. These painters attached to the Emperor's court at Kyōto, still, in Hokusai's day, relied on the formula that had held good for members of the school since the twelfth century, loading the figures of a ceremonial court world with heavy ornate garments that are delineated with the enamelled finish of a miniaturist. Hokusai's set of prints, published about 1810, are remarkable for the closeness with which he approaches, in the colour-print medium, the clear, bright colouring of the Tosa painters (Plate V).

To this year, or shortly afterwards, can be assigned a few more typically Ukiyo-ye prints. There are a few prints of an unusual shape, nearer the *kakemono-ye* size than the normal sheet, one of which I am able to reproduce (Fig. 35). This, and two others reproduced in the Vignier and Inada Catalogue, show an unusual mannerism in the brushwork, not altogether pleasant in the woodcut translation. Of the same date, judging by the signature, is a five-sheet print that has a certain renown more from its rarity and its subject matter than for its beauty. It represents, with a mass of confusing detail, the interior of one of the most famous of the Green-Houses, the House of the Fan, *en fête* for New Year's day.[1] The entire activities, daytime activities that is, of these elegant apartments are depicted from the kitchen to the shrine, from the *sake* store under the stairs to the recess containing the Hō-ō, Bird of Good Omen, painted by Utamaro a decade or so earlier, but there is something stiff and conventional in Hokusai's multitude of courtesans in their finery, and interesting docu

35. Carrying a young girl through a Shintō temple gate for the 'naming ceremony'. *Signed Katsushika Hokusai. About 1810.*

mentary though it may be, it hardly adds to his artistic stature.

In 1812 appeared the first volume of a book called *Ryakugwa haya shinan* ('Quick Lessons in Simplified Drawing'), the first of a number of books designed by Hokusai at different times during his life containing precept and example by way of instruction to would-be artists, or drawings intended as models for craftsmen. Not all of them are to be taken seriously, but here and there some of them give an idea of Hokusai's own practice and as such they are bound to be interesting. The book of 'Quick Lessons' shows how drawings can be made

---

[1]Reproduced in the Ford G. Barclay Sale Catalogue (London 1912).

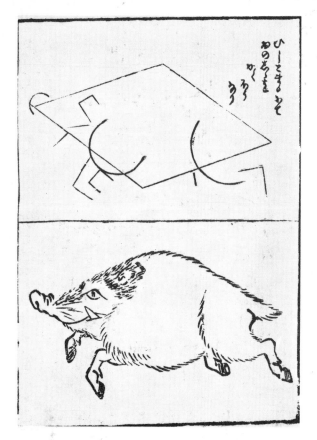

36. Short cuts to drawing a boar. *From* Hokusai Mangwa Hayashinan. *1812.*
37. A page from the 'pictorial dictionary' called *Yehon Hayabiki. 1817.*

with a ruler and a pair of compasses—implements the instructor never needed, we may be sure—and (shades of Cézanne!) even propounds the theory in the preface that 'lines of design consist of circles and squares' (Fig. 36). Other books in this instructional category are *Santai gwafu,* 1816, ('Painting in three forms'), really a drawing book giving pictures of the same objects from three different angles, and *Ippitsu gwafu,* 1823, a book full of delightful drawings made with one stroke of the brush (Figs. 38–9).

But the greatest of the 'drawing-books' was undoubtedly the *Mangwa.* The origin of this vast monument seems to have been the enthusiasm of certain admirers (named Bokusen, Hokutei and Hoku-un) whose acquaintance he made on a visit to the town of Nagoya, all of whom, attracted by the renown of the capital's most talked-of artist, enrolled them-

selves as his pupils. Whilst at Nagoya he threw off, as was customary with him, sheaves of sketches of everything that took his whim, and his followers persuaded him to have a number engraved and published in book form. In Volume I, published eventually in 1814, Hanshū, the writer of the preface, says 'we had the wish that these lessons [the sketches] might be profitable to all those learning to draw, and it was decided to print the drawings in a book. When we asked Hokusai what title he wanted to give to the volume, he said quite simply *Mangwa,* to which we have prefaced his name, thus: *Hokusai Mangwa.*' Many translations of the word *Mangwa* have been put forward, but 'random sketches' or 'miscellaneous sketches' possibly represents Hokusai's intention best (Figs. 40–48).

The idea of publishing a volume of sketches, whether there was any intent to instruct or

V. Ono no Komachi, the Poetess. *One of the series of 'Six Poets'. Signed Katsushika Hokusai. About 1810.*

VI. Kusatsu. *One of the 'Fifty-three Stations of the Tōkaidō'. Unsigned. About 1806.*

 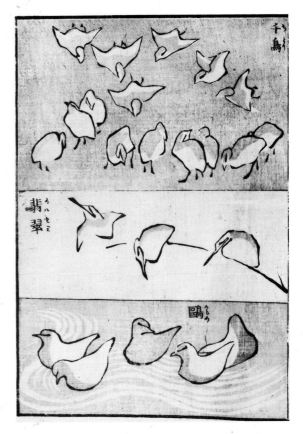

38. Cranes. *From 'Drawings with one stroke of the Brush'. 1823.*
39. Plovers, kingfishers and seagulls. *From 'Drawings with one stroke of the Brush'. 1823.*

not, was by no means a new one in Japan. Many instances could be advanced of compilations of a like kind—Masayoshi's[1] *Shoshoku gwakyō*, 1794, is a very similar gallimaufry of disconnected pictures, in this case obviously intended to provide ideas and exemplars to the craftsmen in ceramics, lacquer or metalwork. But Hokusai's *Mangwa*, beginning with the volume of 1814 and ending with the fifteenth volume published posthumously in 1878, is remarkable for the overwhelming bulk of material—'cette avalanche de dessins, cette débauche de crayonnages', de Goncourt calls it—for the fecundity that could cause one small drawing on a page to proliferate into a score, for the unflagging invention, the

sheer dexterity. Being a collection of sketches, there is no continuity from page to page and even a single page may contain figures from well-known legends mingled higgledy-piggledy with quite inconsequential 'doodles' of birds and fishes. Everything the master drew was considered worthy of perpetuation, and the uncritical homage of pupils, to whom to a certain extent the compilation of these volumes is due, led to the inclusion of much that we can only consider as valueless trifles.

But scattered throughout the volumes there are many splendid things and an impressive anthology could be formed from them. The teeming life of Yedo spills over into his pages, close acquaintance with the people jostling in the streets makes him adept at expressing with a few lines their characteristic gestures, the instinctive movements, and he uses a convention of line that more nearly accords

[1] (1761–1824.) An artist who began his career as a pupil of Shigemasa, but later forsook the Ukiyo-ye style and devoted his energies to book illustration, employing a style that is the epitome of pictorial wit and brevity.

40. A mammoth task. *From vol. 13 of* Mangwa. *About 1849–50.*

with our ideas of naturalism than other Japanese artists. The multitude of sketches too, are instinct with Hokusai's drollery, the caricaturist in him is never very far below the skin, and the foibles of feature and figure in his fellow-countrymen are exaggerated with an impish glee. Occasionally, too, as in the well-known pictures of the jugglers with long noses there is an element of buffoonery, and nobody could complain that Hokusai makes his drawing lessons dull.

Yet one is unwise to look at more than a small fraction of this *magnum opus* at a time. The lack of plan, of homogeneity, in these fifteen volumes, the fragmentary nature of the drawings, succeeds in sating without satisfying, the restlessness of the brush that passes impartially from a mollusc to the Goddess Kwannon, from a hobgoblin to a temple garden, from peonies to pagodas, ends by bewildering us by its very virtuosity. The

many eulogies penned by earlier enthusiasts may have been prompted by this power of Hokusai's to astonish by his inexhaustible variety and virtuosity, but it is difficult to understand how Binyon and Sexton,[1] usually so measured in their judgements, could describe the *Mangwa* as Hokusai's 'masterpiece'. It has something of the power of those other prodigies that so astounded his contemporaries, the Gargantuan Daruma and the miniatures painted on ears of rice, but looked at purely from the artistic standpoint, it yields to several books and to most of the later broadsheets.

In marked contrast is the collection of fifteen prints published under the title of *Shashin gwafu*, 'Pictures drawn from Nature', the preface of which is dated 1814. If the *Mangwa* is the haul of an indiscriminate drag-

[1] *Japanese Colour-Prints*, 1923.

魚濫觀世音

41. The Goddess Kwannon on a giant carp. *From vol. 13 of* Mangwa.

42. Horsemanship. Mangwa, *vol. 6.*

43. Fishers and seaweed gatherers. Mangwa, *vol. 4.*

44. Snow and rain. Mangwa, *vol. 1.*

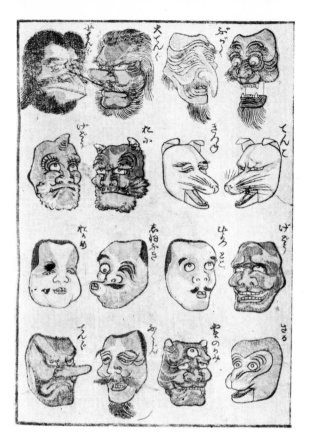

45. A page of masks. Mangwa, *vol. 2.*

46. A page of faces. Mangwa, *vol. 2.*

47. The art of self-defence. Mangwa, *vol. 6.*

48. Contortionists. Mangwa, *vol. 8.*

49. The Buddhist Goddess Kwannon on a dragon. *From* Shashin gwafu. *About 1814.*

net drawn through his incessant output, the *Shashin gwafu* is a selection made with the utmost care to represent at its most brilliant each facet of the artist's genius, and to challenge comparison with the work of any other painter of whatsoever school. His genius for design, for the imaginative interpretation of poetry, is exemplified in the plates of the blossoming plum-branch across a full moon, and the spray of cherry-blossom, both of which represent the apotheosis of the *surimono*

art; the great designers of *kwachō*, with especial reminiscences of the Sōri whose name he took and of that much greater artist, the master Sōtatsu, are evoked by the superb prints of peonies and irises; the workman painting a temple arch, and the philosopher contemplating butterflies, are drawn with the bravura and abandon characteristic of some of the masters of the Kōrin school, and the Kwannon on a dragon is a serious essay in the Kanō style (Fig. 49). But the snowy landscape

50. Lakeside village under snow. *From* Shashin gwafu. *About 1814.*

(Fig. 50), the two mandarin ducks and the pheasant are very much Hokusai's own, magnificently placed upon the page, unerring in their effectiveness, without any taint of the mountebank. This was a book to which the engraver and printer, sensing the importance of the designs, brought their utmost skill and refinement, and the book's present rarity is no doubt due to the original edition having been a very limited one.

The *Mangwa* no doubt set the seal upon Hokusai's popularity with the Yedo public. In these volumes there was something for every taste, and edition followed edition until the blocks were worn out. This popularity seems to have confirmed in Hokusai a rough and somewhat contemptuous attitude towards the polite usages of society, of which boorishness a glimpse had been given in his dealings with Bakin earlier on. Many of the anecdotes that have survived, some of them probably apocryphal, concern his whimsical and even fantastic unsociableness, and from these

stories we get the impression of an eccentric who was humoured by his acquaintances because his failings were seen as the foibles of a genius.

His pride in his position as 'grand maître', at a time when even the leader of the Ukiyo-ye school was of no more account in the social scale than an artisan, is brought out in a number of stories told by people who had known him. One concerns Onoye Baikō, (stage name Kikugorō), one of the leading *kabuki* actors of the day, who had the idea of employing Hokusai's notable talent for drawing spectres in the creation of a scene in a play. He invited the artist to visit him. Actors were considered very low in the social scale—lower even than Ukiyo-ye artists—and Hokusai ignored the invitation. Baikō then decided to visit Hokusai, but finding the artist's room in its customarily filthy state, carefully sat upon a travelling rug that he had brought with him. Hokusai did not deign to notice the actor, but continued with his painting, and the dis-

51. Grating a yam. *One of 'A Hundred Droll Verses in Fashion'. Signed Hokusai. About 1810.*

gruntled actor was forced to leave without even having explained his mission. But so great was his admiration for Hokusai's work, that, swallowing his pride, he made his apologies to the artist, and obtained what he wanted. Moreover, Hokusai showed such magnanimity, that the two became fast friends, and another story relates how Hokusai sold his only mosquito-net in order to raise the money to make a gift to the actor—this was the usual mark of esteem—thereafter enduring nightly torture from mosquitoes until a friend provided him with another net.

One who had known Hokusai's studio told how the artist had painted a large sign upon the walls: 'It is no use bowing and scraping; and it is no use bringing me bribes.' Even

quite important callers were submitted to all sorts of unpleasant indignities. One of the Shōgun's retainers is reported to have called at the artist's studio one day, only to find the artist (no doubt specially for his distinguished caller's benefit), busily engaged in removing fleas from his clothes. It is in keeping with what we know of Hokusai that he should have brutally informed the visitor that he was too busy to attend to him, and equally typical that, the visitor having shown proper respect by waiting until the disinfestation was over, Hokusai should have presented the Shōgun's man with a drawing, though not without a parting injunction that should anyone ask about the condition of the studio, he was to be told what a model of cleanliness it was.

CHAPTER FIVE

THE GREAT LANDSCAPE AND KWACHŌ PRINTS

1820-1832

As the decade from 1810 to 1820 was devoted largely to book illustration, so the next decade was given up in great part, though not exclusively, to the production of the landscape and bird-and-flower colour-prints, prints which we now consider Hokusai's greatest works. The years were not entirely barren in book illustrations: the books of designs for craftsmen represent a new activity of the tireless artist (now in his seventh decade), the *Suikoden,* a collection of pictures without text published soon after the completion of the translation of this famous Chinese novel (Fig. 89), is a fine collection of drawings in the 'Chinese' style, and the *Yehon Teikin Orai,* the illustrated 'Communication of Home Precepts', has many delightful pages. But the books fall into insignificance in comparison with the magnificent succession of colour-prints that appeared during the period.

To appreciate the especial achievement of Hokusai in landscape these prints have to be viewed with the dual vision advocated in the Introduction: with the native eye, familiar with a gallery of Japanese and Chinese landscapes to which each of the previous six centuries had contributed; and our own, used to the canvases of such artists as Rubens, Claude, Poussin, Turner, Constable and Cézanne. In Japan, landscape has always been the master art of painting; there, the greatest artists did not express themselves, as in Europe, through compositions based on human forms, but by visions of toppling crag and misty lake, of wooded hills fading into remote distance, of the sea congealed into monumental curves. Man, if he appeared at all, was made to appear the accident he is upon the earth's crust, a diminutive creature crossing the frail bridge he has thrown from precipice to precipice, or becalmed in a tiny boat in the midst of a lake without boundaries.

The last thing their landscapes were intended to convey was a picture of some locality: that would have reduced the universal poetry they sought to express to parochial prose. Topography meant no more to them than perspective, there were guide books enough if it was information that was required. These painters were carrying the soul upon a journey, and mundane matters, matter-of-fact sign-posts, could only be a hindrance and thwart the flight of the spirit. In the country of the mind there were no tea-houses or pleasure-beaches. The accidents of weather and time, too, were too ephemeral to be fit subject for the painter-philosophers, their landscapes were bathed in a light that never was on sea or land and that cast no shadows, the rise and set of luminaries, sun or moon or planet unknown to us, was recorded to mark not the hour of the day but the passage of cosmic time. In short the weather and the locality, so vital in our landscape, were of little account to the Japanese landscapist of the classic periods: manner was everything, the ink laid on here in brush strokes strong and wiry, and there in a moist haze that caressed the silk or paper, the artist exerting all his skill with the brush to evoke the response of those trained to comprehend the language of brushwork, which we find as difficult to appreciate as that other allied art of theirs, chirography.

In the art of Ukiyo-ye, directed to people who were usually without the upbringing that would have given them an understanding of this kind of landscape painting, and finding its subject in the gayer activities of the people, there was at first little room for landscape at all, except as lightly indicated backgrounds to the figures; nor did the woodcut medium, with its uncompromisingly clear-cut outlines, lend itself to the subtle gradations of tone, and the *nōtan,* that constituted much of the beauty of the classical Kanō or Chinese landscape. There *were* artists in the Ukiyo-ye school who gave evidence of a knowledge of the aristocratic styles of painting, but usually their own versions rose no higher than deliberate parody or burlesque, this 'guying' of the Grand Manner being one of the jests most appreciated by the Yedo commoners. Occasionally there were quite sincere attempts at landscape, Kiyomasu quite early in the eighteenth century designing sets of 'Eight Views of Ōmi' and 'The Four Seasons', but these are in a Tosa convention, and the rather crude engraving and the hand-applied colours make them more 'Primitive' than the paintings of hundreds of years earlier.

The Ukiyo-ye masters of the last quarter of the eighteenth century were, however, of different clay to those of fifty years earlier, and a few might have been capable of vying with the masters of the established academies. Many of the prints of Kiyonaga, Yeishi and Utamaro are of *plein-air* nature, and often lovely snatches of the countryside or of Yedo set the scene for the figures which are always the main subject. In some albums of poetry published about 1790, Utamaro actually included a few plates that are pure landscape, including one remarkable essay in the Kanō style.[1] But the Ukiyo-ye artists are frankly materialistic; the places they depict are real places, known to the Yedo artisans and shopkeepers who bought the colour-prints. The old anonymity is gone. Now every locality has

its proper name, and the print-makers delight in bringing in places well-known to the public, the Enoshima beach, the Yoshiwara, the Sumida River, dwelling upon features by which each district was recognized, like the Cushion-pine in Aoyama, the Castle at Ōsaka, the Water-wheel at Onden.

Meisho-ki, 'Records of Famous Places', supplied this need of the populace for information of places of interest, but these little books were rarely of any great artistic value, they were useful guides in which the pictures were little more than diagrams, with the names of temples and towns in cartouches dotted over the pages. Besides these, other little books, called 'Pleasures of the East', 'Yedo Sparrows' or 'Souvenirs of the Capital' or by some such fanciful title, gave a series of pictures, of which the public never tired, of the life in the capital, the daily commerce of the streets, or picnic parties in the country suburbs, and by the time of Utamaro they had become the vehicle for landscape prints, albeit on a small scale, when such a thing was almost unknown in broadsheet form. Hokusai's quartet of books described in Chapter III, 'Amusements of the East', 'Fine Views of the Eastern Capital', 'Range upon Range of Mountains' and 'Both Banks of the Sumida River' are simply a development of these pleasant volumes. It is true that Hokusai's books originated in the suites of comic poems that accompany the designs, but the poems are really only incidental to the prints, and never divert him from his aim, which was the depiction of the well-known landmarks and the people's activities in and around them. The pictures are still 'figures with landscapes' rather than 'landscapes with figures'.

It is a long way from the 'Both Banks of the Sumida River' to the 'Thirty-six Views of Fuji', but links do exist, mainly in the form of book illustrations, from 1806, the date of the second broadsheet 'Chūshingura' set, to 1823, the date of the first of the 'Thirty-six Views'. The backgrounds to this series of Chūshingura prints already show some of the character-

---

[1] *Kyōgetsu-bō.* 1789. Odes on the moon, with five appropriate designs.

.52. Waves and birds. *A 'blue print'. About 1825.*

53. Blind men fording a stream. *From* Hokusai Sōgwa. *1820.*

istics of the later work, both in the brushwork and in the colour, and throughout the volumes of the *Mangwa* there are drawings that combine a growing expressiveness in the line with a new mastery in design. The snow-landscape in the *Shashin gwafu* of about 1814 (Fig. 50) is also a pointer, and in two volumes of 1819 and 1820, the *Hokusai Gwashiki* (Figs. 54–5) and the *Hokusai Sōgwa* (Fig. 53) there are half a dozen landscapes (besides a number of other very fine things) that have all the elements, save colour, of the great prints soon to be produced. The drawing impresses by an eloquent simplicity, and the use of flat tints enhances the grandeur of the composition. Every detail that might distract from the sweep of the lines, from the weight of the mountain masses, from the desolation of the waste of waters, is purged away.

The lovely 'Fuji in Clear Weather' (Plate VII) is a logical development in colour of the *Gwashiki* and *Sōgwa* designs. There is the same calm selection of the lines most calculated to give the broadest effect, and the few colours, graduated in a manner especial to the wood-block-printer's art, conduce to a sublimity that few other landscapes in the world attain to. Hokusai, we know, was familiar with styles of painting of schools other than the Ukiyo-ye and may have aspired to lift the humble woodcut to a place beside the masterpieces of the Kanō and Chinese schools. Certainly, the 'Thirty-six Views' and the other series of prints produced about the same time, were far from being in the Ukiyo-ye tradition: the aim often soars above the materialistic Ukiyo-ye level, the trivial affairs of men and women forgotten for once, or viewed with a Godlike

54. Village under snow. *From the* Hokusai Gwashiki. *1819.*

55. Snowy landscape with a mountain torrent. *From the same book as last.*

56. Travellers on the Tōkaidō at Hodogaya. *One of the 'Thirty-six Views of Fuji'.*

57. A high wind in Yeigiri. *Same set as last.*

58. The timber yard, Tatekawa, Honjō. *Same set as last.*

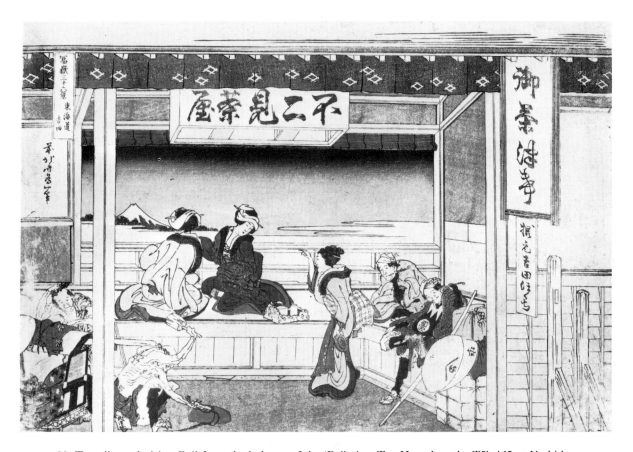

59. Travellers admiring Fuji from the balcony of the 'Fuji-view Tea House' on the Tōkaidō at Yoshida.
Same set as last.

detachment against a background of the elemental forms and forces of nature, and dwarfed by the eternal cone of Fuji, which, near or far, hints at the transitoriness of human life.

But in electing to design the 'Thirty-six Views of Fuji', Hokusai was also pledging himself to satisfy the demand of the Yedo merchants, artisans and others forming the *heimin,* the common folk—people with an avidity for travel, especially in the purlieus of the Capital—for pictures of the places they had visited, a demand that had till then been met by the *meisho-ki* and books such as Hokusai's 'Fine Views of the Eastern Capital'. Nothing comparable in broadsheet form, if we except a few prints by Toyohiro (1763–1828) had been published before; indeed, we can look upon the undertaking as a daring innovation.

Hokusai's prints (Figs. 56–65) lie between two opposing styles, that of the Japanese of the ancient schools, suggesting by evocative arrangements in monochrome a landscape of the imagination, and that of our own western landscapists, approaching as near as the oil or watercolour mediums will allow to a realistic representation of a certain place at a certain date and time. The compromise is one that allowed free play to Hokusai's genius for design, for composition: although his intent, expressed by a descriptive label on each print, was to depict a known locality, or Fuji from a familiar vantage point, the depiction is mainly incidental, the overriding consideration has been the pattern, the possibilities of the scene from the colour-print viewpoint. There is a lack of insistence upon the identifying detail, either of contour or colour, since such an emphasis would have destroyed the unity of impression that is his paramount aim. The 'Fuji in Clear Weather' is a perfect example: it is the essential Fuji, every distracting and insignificant detail shorn away (Plate VII)

It says much for the responsiveness of the print-buying public in Japan at the time, that this original form of landscape could be assimilated and applauded, that it could enjoy Hokusai's harmonizing of old and new elements, his representation of places to which they could give a name in a style that recalled the majestic indifference to locality of the old Masters, and in a medium that translated the evocative, brush-applied washes of the ancients into block-printed colours, of which a strong blue, new to the printer's range of tints, and various other bold colours were orchestrated into strident chords. To us, with a background (up to the time of Hokusai's impact upon Europe) of a representational method of landscape painting culminating in the quasi-scientific experiments of the Impressionists, his prints seemed to have achieved at a bound that compromise between the representation of actuality on the one hand, and the creation of an abstract design in colour and line satisfying in itself on the other, that was the eternal problem of Cézanne and of many artists since.

Not all of the prints in the Fuji set are successful. In some, the retention of the conventional bars of cloud, a Tosa artifice, is an anachronism, a survival that does not blend with the new idiom. In others, there is a too obvious straining after effect either in the foreground incident (the old cooper caulking a huge barrel is a case in point) or else in the conventions used for landscape feature—the waves of the Kanaya Ford on the Tōkaidō for example (Fig. 64). But these apart, how rich the series is in magnificent prints!

The set, which actually numbers forty-six views, a supplementary ten having been added of views from the districts beyond Yedo on the other side of the mountain, appeared at intervals between 1823 and 1829, and from the differences in printing, the variations of colour in prints that are obviously early impressions, it has been assumed that the artist actually supervised the printing of the first issues. Their popularity led to repeated editions being printed long after the blocks had ceased to yield worthwhile impressions,

VII. Fuji in clear weather. One of the 'Thirty-six Views of Fuji'.

VIII. Fuji seen between the hillocks of Lower Meguro, terraced for vegetable growing. *Same set as last.*

IX. Moonlight on the Yodo River. *From the set of 'Snow—Moon—Flowers'.*

X. The 'Coast of Seven Leagues' (Shichiri-ga-hama) in Sōshū province. *Designed entirely in varying shades of blue. From same set as last.*

60. Fuji from Umedawa, in Sōshū province. *One of the 'Thirty-six Views of Fuji'.*

61. Fuji above the lightning. *Same set as last.*

62. Fuji from the Nihon Bridge, Yedo. *Same set as last.*

63. The flowering cherry-trees at Gotenyama on the Sumida River. *Same set as last.*

64. The Kanaya Ford on the Tōkaidō. *Same set as last.*

65. The hollow of the deep-sea wave. *Same set as last.*

66. The 'Bridge of the Brocade Sash' in the Province of Suō. *From the set of 'Bridges'.*

and these pale ghosts give a completely false notion of the prints in their finest state.

Whilst this magnificent series was being published, Hokusai began others, and the 'Waterfalls', the 'Bridges', the 'Lū-Chū Islands', the 'Snow, Moon, Flowers' and both the 'Bird and Flower' series are all thought to have appeared between 1827 and 1830 or soon after.

The 'Waterfalls' (Plate XI; Fig. 69) can be called, in some ways, the most inimitable of all Hokusai's prints: they are idiosyncratic to a degree, powerful in conception, masterly in design, with something extravagant and even bizarre in the daring conventions he employs to suggest the mass of falling water in each print. The title of the set of eight—'Travelling Around the Waterfall Country'—is again one to appeal to town-dwellers with a wander-lust, and as such one might have expected some concessions to topography. But Hokusai merely accepts the waterfall as a theme on which to build a set of superb variations, the very limitations of the thematic material, the column of descending water, or the rock-wandering cascade, so uncompromising in their lines, challenging the artist to his greatest feats of synthesis, of bringing order out of the chaotic elements of nature. Perhaps he was spurred by remembrance of the painting of the 'Nachi Waterfall' tradition-ally ascribed to the almost legendary 'father of Japanese painting' Kanaoka (second half of the ninth century) in which the same dramatic cleavage of the design is achieved by the waterfall as it is in Hokusai's 'Amida Fall' (Plate XI). Seen hanging together, as five of the 'Waterfall' prints were in the 1948 British Museum Exhibition, there was no more impressive tribute on the walls to the artist's genius. The unity of the colour-scheme throughout, limited, with minor exceptions, to tones of blue, cold and warm green, maroon and yellow, the uniformity of the format, the similarity of the subject-matter, aided the idea of the artist improvising on a given theme, unafraid of jarring dissonances in the search for the ultimate resolving chord of design.

The 'Bridges' have, by some, been rather faintly praised in comparison with the 'Fuji' and 'Waterfall' prints. It is true that the series does not contain any monumental design of the order of the 'Fuji in Clear Weather' or 'The Wave', and this seems only to reinforce the argument that the greater the topographi-cal accuracy, the less the chance of evolving a design completely satisfying in itself. For in this set, Hokusai was obviously bent on portraying the particular bridge instead of the typical bridge. There is a greater attention to the identifying detail, to the picturesque effect. He causes us to catch our breath at the appalling chasm that the couple are intrep-idly crossing by the 'Hanging Bridge' of bamboo and cord, we are intrigued by the extravagant shape of the Drum Bridge at the Tenjin shrine entailing so arduous an ascent, and marvel like any other sightseer at the Festival of Lanterns in Ōsaka (Fig. 70). Tied though he may be to his subject, and restriction though that may be on his scope, he was obviously intensely interested in the 'Bridges' and some of his most entertaining prints are the result, prints that show the sort of urbanity that comes from a perfect mastery of the medium. The 'Bridge of Boats', a most accomplished snowscape, is perhaps the finest of the set, and I am able to reproduce the very rare first edition of this print[1] (Plate XV).

Another series of landscape designs of the same order as those described above is that forming one of the groupings so affected by the Japanese. In *Setsu-gekkwa*, 'Snow, Moon, Flowers', one print is dedicated to each of these objects of worship among a nation of nature-lovers. Hokusai is never quite the poet of moonlight that his young contemporary Hiroshige was to prove; he used it as an adjunct to formal composition rather than as the source of a magical atmospheric effect;

---

[1] Formerly in the collection of the late Charles Rowe, Esq., and now in the Bristol City Art Gallery.

67. Pines and waves in Ryūdo, the Dragon's Cave. *One of the 'Eight Views of the Lū-Chū Islands'.*

68. Irises. *From the set of 'Large Flowers'.*

69. Kirifuri Fall in Kurokami Mountain. *One of the set of 'Waterfalls'.*

XI. The Waterfall of Amida (*so called from the resemblance of the round hollow worn in the cliff to the head of Amida Buddha*).
From the set of 'Waterfalls'.

XII. Crossbill and thistle. *From the set of 'Small Flowers'.*

XIII. Chrysanthemums. *From the set of 'Large Flowers'.*

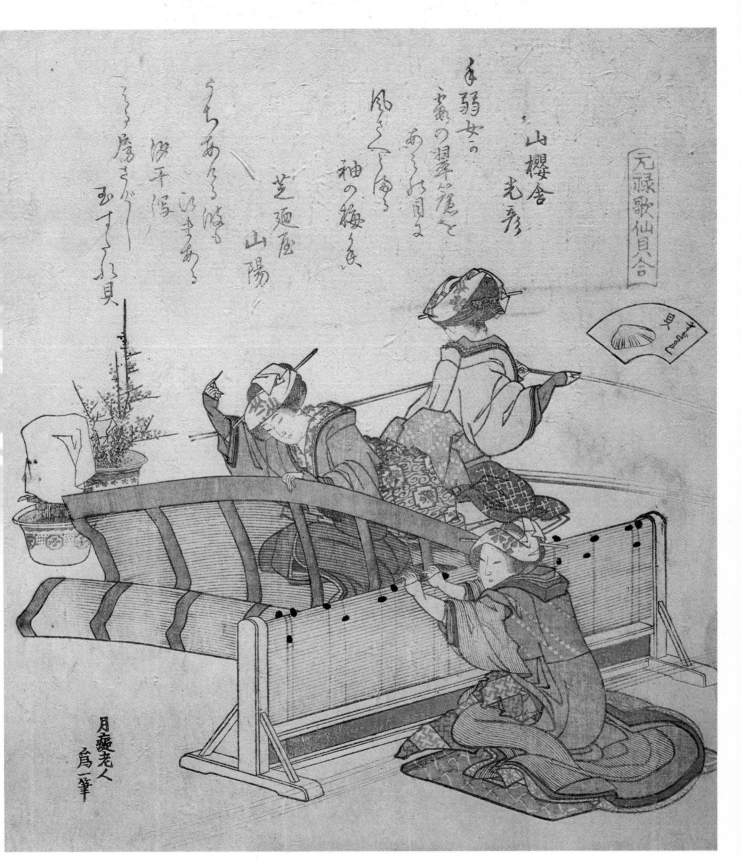

XIV. Girls making bamboo blinds. *A surimono. About 1824.*

XV. The 'Bridge of Boats' at Sano, Province of Kōzuke. *From the set of 'Bridges'.*

70. Evening of the Festival of Lanterns, Temma Bridge, Settsu. *From the set of 'Bridges'.*

but in the 'Moonlight on the Yodo River' despite the repetition of the 'Moon's round O', in the title-label, and the conventional bands of mist, the white light on the water and the plying boats is real enough and the print on the whole a captivating one (Plate X). The 'Snow Scene on the Sumida' and 'Blossom at Yoshino' complete a trio that have to perfection this conveyance of the actuality of a scene without sacrifice of the formal harmony.

Quite different, however, is the set of 'Eight Views of the Lū-Chū Islands' (Fig. 67) and did they not bear the same signature as the other prints produced about this time (all the great landscape and *kwachō* prints are signed *Zen* (formerly) Hokusai I-Itsu) one would be inclined to place them in a different period altogether: perhaps they came at the end of this particular bout of intense activity, shortly after 1830. Binyon and Sexton thought it possible that he had based the drawings on 'sketches or descriptions by another hand' and mention their 'free and a little fantastic composition' which we would expect from the artist in the circumstances. There is little variation in the colouring of the prints, blue and green predominate with little touches of yellow and brown or red, very effective use being made of the white of the paper itself. From another hand than Hokusai's they would probably have come in for a greater meed of praise, but charming as they are, there is a certain quietness, even perhaps tameness, about them that has always left them in comparative obscurity.

At the same time as these notable landscape prints were being published, Hokusai also designed two wonderful sets of 'Flowers and Birds', known from the size of the sheets as the 'Small Flowers' (Plate XII; Fig. 71) and the 'Large Flowers' (Plate XIII; Fig. 68). Each set consists of ten prints.

Our response to these prints is immediate, no former acquaintance with or study of the theory and practice of painting in the Far East has to precede an appreciation of these enchanting compositions, and our delight is spontaneous. Yet that selection from the maze of lines and colours in nature of those most effective on the page is as uncompromising in these *kwachō* as it is in the landscapes; the spray of weeping cherry-flowers is no less conventionalized to fit the artist's scheme of design than the Kirifuri Waterfall, the colour is no less arbitrarily used on the petals of the lily than on the cone of Fuji. Perhaps we come to these compositions half-prepared for the manner of the East, for whilst we have invariably drawn the human figure and landscape with 'truth to nature', it has been customary from our earliest efforts to draw at all to conventionalize flowers and leaves, and most of our formal pattern, in book, or on textile and ceramic, has been of this kind. But this can only in part explain our immediate reaction.

Hokusai takes advantage of the bright colour of his subjects to use a fuller palette than is normal to him, and surprises by brilliant effects—the weeping cherry and bullfinch are against a background of a vivid but dark blue, the bird and flower-spray seem caught in a dazzling beam against a summer night sky (Fig. 71); the cuckoo and azalea have instead the bright blue of a spring morning behind them.

Lovely as his *kwachō* prints are, Hokusai was not so much the innovator in this form as he was in landscape. There was an immensely long tradition in Japan dating back hundreds of years, the greatest of their masters had excelled in this kind of design, impelled to such a choice of subject by that deep-seated love of living things innate in the Japanese, and the veneration in which certain flowers were held through Buddhistic and other associations, composing them with their brush strokes with the same unerring eye to effect as guided the hands of the masters of the sister art of 'living flower' arrangement, *ikebana*. There was never anything casual in the arrangements: they were the outcome and the expression of a profound culture, a

71. Bullfinch and weeping cherry. *From the set of 'Small Flowers'.*

knowledge of the lore of flowers and of the considerable body of poetry connected with them; and the result of a careful study of the stylization of their forms necessary to bring them into the desired pattern without destroying the impression of life, of motion and lively colour.

Several Ukiyo-ye artists vied with the masters of hallowed name in *kwachō,* invariably with a certain sincerity in their approach that contrasts markedly with the generally flippant way in which they dealt with the old masters' subjects. Harunobu and his contemporary Koryūsai, and later Shigemasa and Utamaro, created *kwachō* that took advantage of the peculiarities of the woodcut medium, the firm line, the gradated mass of colour, the 'blind-printing' that gives the illusion of form without the use of line or colour, and inspired their engravers and printers to interpretive reproduction of the utmost refinement, so that prints of this type are among the greatest

treasures of the Ukiyo-ye heritage. Throughout his life, Hokusai showed a leaning towards subjects of this nature, books like the *Shashin gwafu,* the *Gwashiki* and *Sōgwa,* and, of course, the *Mangwa,* have many wonderful pages of 'birds and flowers'.

But these two sets of separately issued *kwachō* are unquestionably his finest works of the type, and excepting the three most famous of the Fuji series, are the most universally popular of any of his prints. If they have a fault, in our eyes, it is a certain overstylization in the forms of the birds, which gradually, throughout his career, evolve more and more towards a recognizably Hokusai-ish species (Fenollosa complains that they 'all have the same uncanny expression') but it is easy to forgive so minor a blemish. The best of these prints have a serenity of conception and design that links them with the noblest of the landscape prints, a beauty that lifts them on to a plane where they are in company with the greatest paintings of the world.

In this vastly productive period, Hokusai still found time to design *surimono* (Figs. 72–4; Plate XIV), though far less prolifically than before. One series, about 1822, entitled *Genroku Kasen Kai awase* ('Choice Collection of Verse on Shells'), recognizable by the little design of shells on a fan placed below the title, is of especial beauty, the example reproduced giving some idea of the delicacy of the work, the enormous contrast with the book illustrations of the same time. Another set, issued for the Horse Year 1822 shows how superbly Hokusai could manage compositions in what we call 'still life', and helps to illustrate the many-sidedness of the talent that makes him the despair of monographists with no more than one volume at their disposal.[1]

In accounting for the prodigious labours of these years, it is easy to lose sight of Hokusai's life during the period; indeed, one comes to

[1]Entitled *Umazukushi,* 'The Ubiquitous Horse'. With the 25 prints that, by one association or other, punning or otherwise, bring in an allusion to the Horse, went a triptych of the Sumida River.

72. A fisherman watching the moon. Possibly a self-portrait. *A surimono. About 1835.*

identify it with his work, there would seem to have been no room for anything else. Few men can have been so little affected by the events in the world around them. Japan in the first forty years of the nineteenth century, under ineffectual and dissolute Tokugawa Shōguns, was a country that vacillated between periods of comparative prosperity and of utter famine, between phases of unbridled licence in manners and morals, and of rigorous counter-measures given effect in sumptuary edicts. It was an uncertain world at best, and the

73. A girl making a model of Fuji. *A surimono. About 1824.*

instability of the times is exposed as much in the literature of the period as in the uprisings of the common people from time to time recorded by the historians. The art purveyed for the common people in Yedo and Ōsaka by the Ukiyo-ye artists was, on the whole, a degenerate version of the finely designed and printed work that had been published before 1800, and bespoke a change in the character of the people for whom it was produced, a slackening of the fibres, a weakening of critical discernment.

But Hokusai maintained his own standards in a world of changing values, and seemed to possess a sort of inner integrity as regards his art, quite beyond the reach of the most momentous events in the world around him. In this immunity he reminds one—as he reminds one in other ways, by his uncouthness, his physical stamina, and his incessant output—of his contemporary Turner, whose art similarly showed little sign of the stress of the times he lived in and was only affected by the great crises of the Napoleonic wars to the extent that they limited travel on the continent.

Yet Hokusai was a man, if not like other men, at least with some of their needs, and many of their tribulations, and there is a mellowing in his art, a turning to subjects of deeper import in his later years, that bespeaks an 'eye that has looked on man's mortality'.

Between the time of his momentous visit to Nagoya in 1812 and the commencement of the 'Thirty-six Views' about 1823, he travelled extensively, and there are records of his having stayed in both Ōsaka and Kyōto. His visit to Ōsaka resulted in a number of local artists enrolling themselves as his pupils, but at Kyōto, the centre of the schools of classical and aristocratic painting, he made little impression. His work was interrupted by a serious illness about 1828 or 1829, of which he cured himself with a concoction made according to an old Chinese recipe, and again in 1834 when he was forced to leave Yedo for some obscure reasons connected with the misdemeanours of a scapegrace grandson. Although Hokusai married twice, little is known of his wives, except that they were both separated from him, either by divorce or death. He was hardly more fortunate in his children, two sons and three daughters. One son came into the old mirror-making business and was a continual source of trouble to his father; the other seems to have had some minor post as a government official. One daughter died early; the youngest, Oyei, an artist of some talent, divorced her husband and looked after Hokusai in his old age, proving, from all accounts, a devoted companion; the third married Yanagawa Shigenobu, one of Hokusai's best pupils, and was

74. Still life—soup bowls, napkin, box of chopsticks, black beans and *gomanei* (a dried sardine-like fish). *A surimono. 1822.*

the mother of the child who caused so much embarrassment to the old painter and who appears to have been responsible for Hokusai's need to leave the capital.

Hokusai's exile, in the distant town of Uraga, lasted from 1834 until 1836, and several informative and occasionally pathetic letters written to his publishers have survived of this unhappy period. They show him just as we would have expected to find him: even in a strange place, friendless and with hardly the bare necessities of existence, completely absorbed in his work, anxious to impress upon his publishers the need to employ the most expert wood-engraver, Yegawa Tomekichi, to cut the blocks for his next book; giving minute instructions for printing monochrome illustrations, with a homely comparison of the clear Chinese ink tone to shellfish soup, and of the deeper-toned Chinese ink to the thickness of haricot soup; inveighing against some of the malpractices of engravers.

In the first letter, written in 1834, he wrote 'As to your "old 'un", it is always the same, the power of his brush continues to grow, and more than ever to work industriously. When he is one hundred, he will be numbered among the great artists.' In the same letter is his request that Yegawa should engrave his 'Warrior' book (possibly *Yehon Sakigake,* which was published in 1836). 'The reason I hold absolutely that the engraving should be done by Yegawa is this', he writes, 'that well as the *Mangwa* and the "Poets" were engraved, they are far from having the perfection of the "Fuji" book engraved by him.' He ends, 'What I ask is the sharpness of his execution, and this would be a satisfaction to a poor old man who hasn't much further to go.' And at this place in the original letter, Hokusai sketched himself as an old merchant supported on two paint brushes instead of crutches.

In the last letter to survive from his period in exile, written in early 1836, there is evidence of the misery in which he was being forced to live. 'In this cruel season', he wrote, 'above all when travelling, there is nothing but hard times, and among other things, having to endure the great coldness with no more than a single garment, at my age of seventy-six years. I beg you to think of the sad condition in which I exist; but my arms [and here he sketched them] are as strong as ever, and I am working furiously. My one aim is to become a great artist.' However cast down by his wretched mode of existence, he was thinking all the time of his work. A sudden thought came into his head as he wrote the

letter just quoted, and he scribbled a P.S. 'I must ask the engraver not to add an eyelid where I do not put one; and as for noses, these are not mine [here he sketched a nose full-face and profile], and those which are usually engraved are the noses of the Utagawas[1] which I do not like at all, and which are contrary to the rules of drawing. It is also the fashion to draw eyes thus [inserting here a drawing of eyes with a black point at the centre], but I do not like these eyes any more than the noses.' And he ends this letter with another afterthought, like a sigh: 'As for my life, it is no longer in the public eye, and I cannot give you my address.'

His return to the capital coincided with a great famine, which he contrived to survive by dint of an incredible output of paintings and drawings, not a few of which are, no doubt, in that vast corpus of drawings 'attributed to Hokusai' in every collection of Japanese art. In 1839 he suffered the calamity he had feared all his life, the loss of his paintings and drawings in a fire. The old man who bragged of the number of times he had changed house to escape this common enemy of Yedo-dwellers—he is supposed to have moved over ninety times—must have been desolated by his loss, but it served only to spur him on to greater efforts, as the numerous paintings dating from 1839, when he was on the threshold of his ninth decade, testify.

---

[1] The family to which Kunisada and Kuniyoshi and many others belonged.

CHAPTER SIX

PAINTINGS AND DRAWINGS

IN considering the *oeuvre* of any of the major Ukiyo-ye artists, their paintings, as distinct from their designs for prints, are apt to fall into the background, partly because of their rarity and the inaccessibility of those that do exist, partly because the technique and format interpose more obstacles to our appreciation than the prints. Indeed, there are those European critics who consider the paintings to be of little consequence, arguing that it is only the prints that have any especial artistic significance for us. Unquestionably, none of Hokusai's paintings has anything like the effectiveness, to our eye, of the finest of his landscape and bird-and-flower colour-prints, but may this not be due to some extent to our lack of sympathy with the eastern idiom of painting, its reliance on quite other ways of expression than those we have come to appreciate in western paintings? Although they are known to us mainly through their colour-prints, Hokusai and many other Ukiyo-ye artists were, first and foremost, painters. They set great store upon their *nikuhitsu*, 'autograph paintings', their 'diploma' works were in this rather than in any other form, and we shall never understand the Japanese view of their stature as artists unless an attempt is made to assess their work in the brush medium.

The critical assessment of Hokusai's painting still rests, and is likely to rest, on the work of Fenollosa, who had unparalleled opportunities for the study of an immense and mostly authentic bulk of Hokusai's paintings and drawings, brought together, first in Boston, where in 1893 an exhibition was held of nearly two hundred examples mainly drawn from the Bigelow collection, and again, in Tōkyō, where in 1900 the greatest exhibition of works in the brush medium was held, no fewer than two hundred and seventy works, many of major importance, being hung. In the Catalogue, Fenollosa wrote of the latter exhibition 'From it a minute determination of the rapid changes in Hokusai's style has been rendered possible; upon it, as a prime authority, will have to depend the world's critical study of Hokusai's artistic work in future centuries.' This catalogue does, indeed, remain the most valuable contribution to the study of Hokusai's work, and we may count ourselves fortunate that its preparation and that of the earlier Boston catalogue too, was entrusted to one of the most enlightened of western lovers of Japanese art.

Usually, paintings seem to have been commissioned by the wealthier of the artists' patrons and, especially where they were the work of an artist making his way, they show the careful finish, the painstaking technique, of one intending to make his mark, and a certain restraint in the choice of the subject-matter, a curbing of the fancifulness that may inform the same artist's colour-prints.

The few paintings known of Hokusai's early days are of this order. The 'Courtesan and Attendants', signed Sōri, is a very lovely example, dating about 1797–8 (Fig. 78). In technique it is entirely in the Ukiyo-ye tradition. There is a firm flowing outline that swells and dwindles without the *bravura* that the more impetuous brush of a Kanō master would have given; detailed dress patterns and scrupulously rendered coiffures; bright and opaque colour, with the flesh-parts of a

75. Two Beauties.
Brush-painting. Signed Gwakyōjin Hokusai. About 1802.
Hakone Gallery, Japan.

76. Shishi Lions in black on a gold screen. *Signed Gwakyōjin Hokusai. About 1800–4.* Tōkyō National Museum.

77. Tametomo, the archer of fabulous strength, attacked by demons when he lands on their island. *Brush-painting. 1811.* British Museum.

uniform dead pallor, or with the slightest tinge of pink beneath the brows. Technique apart, however, the painting is one of great individuality. The forms and features of the girls are what we know so well from the prints under the signature of Sōri, indeed the girl whose head appears in the *surimono* 'A Souvenir from the Shrine of Benten' (Fig. 13) might easily have been the model for the courtesan in the painting. Tajima[1] reproduces another painting of obvious kinship with this, 'A Beautiful Woman and a Small Monkey', signed Hyakurin Sōri and sealed Sōri, and it is difficult to see why he should ascribe it to the pupil of Hokusai who took over the art-name Sōri when Hokusai discarded it. The confusion that exists concerning the paintings of the various artists using the name Sōri makes it dangerous to dogmatize on the questions of signatures and seals, but judging by the style alone, the 'Beautiful Woman and Small Monkey' seems to be a particularly fine painting by Hokusai in the last years of the eighteenth century. The 'Two Beauties' in the Hakone Gallery (Fig. 75) is another typical painting of the period.

Even at this early period, Hokusai did not confine himself to the Ukiyo-ye style—the fine screen of Shishi Lions in the Tōkyō National Museum (Fig. 76) proves his ability to adopt a freer manner when occasion demanded—but it is a noticeable fact that he was, as a painter, able to hark back to the 'typical' Ukiyo-ye style, especially for such subjects as 'beautiful women', when his book illustrations and prints were diverging more and more from that norm. But side by side with the orthodox paintings there are others that keep pace with and outstrip the originality that marks his work for the engravers. 'Tametomo and the Demons' (Fig. 77) was painted in 1811 for Bakin, whose novel of Tametomo, *Chinsetsu Yumihari Zuki*, Hokusai illustrated about this time, and gives evidence of the Chinese influences that imbued the

[1]*Masterpieces Selected from the Ukiyo-ye School*, Vol. IV, 1908.

78. Courtesan and attendants.
Brush-painting. Signed Sōri. About 1798.
Museum of Fine Arts, Boston.

drawings for the *Suikoden*, and of the diablerie that was the product of the artist's own fantastic mind. But the painting is in a curiously mixed style, the trees and birds in

79. Head of Daruma. *Brush-painting. About 1842–5.*
British Museum.

la dernière étape de l'art national sans mélange extérieur': beyond this point, the artist must have trespassed on the domain of western oil and watercolour painters. That he was conscious of the essential difference between Japanese and European painting we can gather from a passage in one of his books on painting, the *Yehon Saishiki Tsū*, 'Treatise on Colouring', in which he wrote concerning the Dutch method of painting in oils, 'We render the form and colour without indicating relief, but in the European method, they attempt to give relief and to deceive our eyes.'

But though paintings showing evidence of a flirtation with alien methods exist, Hokusai's innovations in brushwork were a natural development of his innate fluency in draughtsmanship, a progression towards a freer use of the brush, and of its own individual language, than the enamelled finish of the Ukiyo-ye style permitted. One of his loveliest paintings is a picture painted about 1810–12 known as 'Girls gathering Shells at Ebb-tide'[1] where an exquisite effect is achieved by the intense colour on the dresses of the girls and children at the water's edge in a landscape where atmosphere and distance are suggested by aerial perspective, washes of colour being used much as one of our own watercolourists might have used them.

Later still, Hokusai painted with an entirely uninhibited brush using transparent washes rather than opaque colours, and such paintings can in no sense be classified as Ukiyo-ye in style; rather they recall, without actually imitating, the Kanō and Shijō styles, the first with its emphasis on the eloquent brush strokes, the other, with its approach towards naturalism. The mountainous landscape (Fig. 95) is an example of this eclecticism, the horse and figures in the foreground being Hokusai's own brand of Ukiyo-ye, the distant landscape in something approaching the style of the old masters of the Chinese school. But there is a certain impurity in this

the eastern linear style, the bodies of the demons given form by a sort of arbitrary chiaroscuro. Nothing like this had appeared before in Japan: for good or evil, Hokusai was breaking new ground and expanding the technique to encompass new effects of near-naturalism.

It is paintings of this type, no doubt, that led Gonse to conclude that 'Hokusai marque

---

[1] Reproduced in Tajima, *Opus cit.*

mingling of styles that native connoisseurs criticize. Tajima, expressing the Japanese view, complains that 'From the time Hokusai was about fifty years of age [about 1810]...the bad features of this artist's work seem to have increased yearly: he employed unnatural curves and developed unattractive brushwork which became customary in the paintings of his old age.' There are some paintings, certainly, dating from the twenties that we can sense as violating the canons of good taste in brushwork: there is, in particular, the eccentric stroke used for indicating stuffs, a petty, crinkly line that gives the drawing a restless look and which irritates the eye. This idiosyncrasy appears in prints of the same period; it is particularly noticeable in the prints illustrating a notorious erotic book of Hokusai, *Kinoye no Komatsu*, 'Young Pine Shoots'.[1]

But paintings with these defects form only a part of the artist's output: there are a host of other *kakemono* in which the brushwork is as compelling as in the rough sketch on flimsy paper. The British Museum 'A seller of New Year's poems' is dated 1827 (Fig. 80). It marks the beginning of the final phase in Hokusai's development as a painter. There is complete assurance, extraordinary accomplishment, and the style is his own. 'That classic perfection of touch,' wrote Morrison,[2] 'the glory of the ancient painters of China and Japan, that lofty quality which the European eye recognizes so slowly, and commonly not at all—this final perfection was not Hokusai's.' But this is as unreasonable as a complaint that Turner and Constable lack the touch of Titian or Rubens. The art of painting and the outlook of the painter had changed in the passage of the centuries. We should not decry an innovator simply because he deserts the classical ideal. Yet it has always been the habit to condemn Hokusai for apostasy from

80. A seller of New Year's poems.
Brush-painting. Signed Hokusai I-itsu. 1827.
British Museum.

[1]Considering the vast bulk of Hokusai's work, the *erotica* form a far smaller proportion of his work than was usual among the Ukiyo-ye artists.

[2]*The Painters of Japan*, 1911.

the faith of his forbears in painting: whereas the remarkable thing is that for all his modernism, he still revered the old gods, and was the last great Japanese artist, possibly, to effect a satisfactory compromise between the

81. Cock and hen.
Brush-painting. Signed Zen *Hokusai I-itsu. About 1828.*
Hakone Gallery, Japan.

opposing schools of forward-looking western-ization and backward-looking nationalism. The later nineteenth-century artists either simply aped European methods or tediously repeated the formulae of bygone ages.

Hokusai's paintings from this time are invariably interesting, often splendid, creations. In contradistinction to the intense colours, including a brilliant vermilion, of his early paintings there is what Fenollosa described as a 'warm subdued red...contrasted at focal points with a mellow greenish blue, the combination being held together by masses of warm green culminating in spots of pure yellow— his own creation, unlike anything else in Japanese art, the nearest to the rich effects of European oil work.'

After the age of eighty, Hokusai invariably added his age to his signature, and some of his finest works are proved to have been produced in his green old age. In the Boston exhibition there were a number of notable paintings of this period: 'Blackbirds across a spray of willow' (1841); *Yamato-dake-no-Mikato,* the prince of early Japanese legend (1845); and perhaps the finest, 'Fukurokujū' (one of the Seven Gods of Good Fortune) (1845)—works in which Fenollosa remarked the 'raising of *nōtan,* or dark or light mass, to the leading element of the composition and the blending of this in extraordinary broad tones by his adopted scheme of colours...This solemn breadth of colour-*nōtan* is the triumph of the close of Hokusai's career.' The British Museum is equally rich in fine late works, including one of the most famous, the 'Ducks in a Stream', painted when the artist was in his eighty-seventh year (Fig. 82).

As a painter, Hokusai was continually experimenting, and studied deeply the science, as far as it was known in the east, of colouring. In the 'Treatise on Colouring' already mentioned, he gives instructions for the mixing of colours and, if evidence were needed of his care for the mysteries of his craft, apropos of 'black' wrote: 'There is the antique black and the new black, the brilliant and the dull black, black in the light and black in the shade. As for the old black, it has to be mixed with red; for fresh black, with blue; for dull black with white; for brilliant black, it needs the addition of paste; for black in the light, it is necessary to reflect it with grey.' No experimenter can succeed all the time, and Morrison was right when he wrote 'As a colourist he is puzzling. Commonly his colour is very beautiful; sometimes it is rather ordinary; now and again it is hot, or even muddy.' But when he continues: 'In his brushwork Hokusai was an inventor, a breaker of models, a revolutionist; and no man can throw overboard the teachings of the centuries with impunity', you hear the grudging praise of one who was in love with the ancient masters' works and who, whilst deploring elsewhere the sterility of the academic painters in Hokusai's day, cannot bring himself wholly to admire a style so individual and unorthodox as Hokusai's.

No doubt there will always be controversy as to the merit of Hokusai's paintings, but concerning his drawings and sketches there are, in the west at least, no dissentient voices. They have been praised by people of the most divergent sympathies, by classicist and modern. They have the universal suffrage accorded to the drawings of but few artists, Rembrandt, Leonardo da Vinci and one or two others. There is, for once, a medium comparable with our own—Hokusai uses a brush and Chinese ink on thin paper—and moreover, in the spontaneous sketch, the capture of the fleeting gesture or the bird on the wing, the particular idiom that marks down a painting as oriental is not so much in evidence, since the studied mannerism, the style peculiar to a particular school, was more likely to be manifest when the artist began consciously to *compose* a work.

From one cause and another, and especially the disastrous fire of 1839, the majority of the drawings extant belong to the latter years of the artist's career. They fall into a number of distinct categories. The great bulk are ran-

82. Ducks in a stream.
Brush-painting. 1847.
British Museum.

83. Carnival figure. *Brush-drawing. About 1835–40.* British Museum.

84. Sheet of brush-drawings intended as models for pupils to copy, the drawings being so placed to enable several pupils to work from the sheet at the same time. *About 1835–40.* British Museum.

85. The 'rough first outline that disdains "penning"' (*Fenollosa*).
A sheet of brush studies. About 1822. Freer Gallery, Washington.

dom sketches, as native to the artist as speech. Where an ordinary man might simply observe or reflect, or a writer frame phrases to record an observation or reflection, Hokusai seems always to have had his brush in hand to depict what was passing before his eyes or through his mind. As a consequence, many drawings of this type are too fragmentary to be artistically significant, but often they have an immediacy and a vividness that makes them expressive as few other drawings, east or west, are expressive, the artist compelling us, by the beauty of his line, by his innate feeling for the medium he is using, to take note of his record of trivial happenings, or his unbelievable phantoms, just as another man, because of an eloquent voice, compels us to listen to his everyday remarks.

It is by these unpremeditated sketches, (Figs. 83–7) that we come into the most intimate contact with Hokusai, as we come to know a man from his conversation. From them, even if we knew nothing of his character, we would have deduced an original, an eccentric, or perhaps one should say a humorist, in the old sense of that word. It was not the solid virtues but the foibles of mankind he liked to record, ever ready to seize

on the ridiculous, to raise a laugh at someone's absurdity or misfortune, to portray, without a hint of the moralizer, the follies and the oddities of his fellow-men. And as so often happens with the true humorist, the laughter Hokusai causes is sometimes very close to tears. This vein of humour, an alloy of fun, satire and sympathy, runs through the work of Hokusai in every medium, but comes closest to the surface in his brush drawings.

Other drawings, more studied in their finish, but not designed for print or book illustration, seem to be what might be termed 'presentation drawings', the artist setting himself out to display to the full his draughtsmanship, his virtuosity with the brush. Most of these are figure studies of a mature expressiveness that is more emotional in its appeal than the pure calligraphic brushwork of the ancient masters of Japan, and as moving to us as the drawings of Rembrandt with a reed pen. A fine series of drawings of this order is in the Freer Gallery, two of which are reproduced (Figs. 92–3).

With these, perhaps, may be grouped the drawings in colour-washes, mostly of flowers, birds, shells and kindred natural objects. Hokusai's use of the watercolour medium is

86. Arum leaf and convolvulus. *Brush-drawing*. Victoria and Albert Museum.

87. Revellers. *Brush-drawing*. Freer Gallery, Washington.

88. Orignal drawing from which the engraving (Fig. 89) was prepared. British Museum.

89. A page from the *Suikoden* book of 1829. British Museum.

90. Bringing in osiers. *Brush-drawing for the series 'One Hundred Poems Explained by the Nurse', never engraved. About 1835–9.* British Museum.

91. Three of the 'Heroes of Suikoden'.
Preparatory drawing for the book 'Collection of Pictures of the Heroes of Suikoden', 1829.
British Museum.

92. Tuning the *samisen. Brush-drawing. About 1820–5.*
Freer Gallery, Washington.

93. Girl playing a *samisen. Brush-drawing. About 1820–5.*
Freer Gallery, Washington.

most original, flat washes of colour being used to build up form, with slight strengthening here and there by outlining, much reliance for effect resting on the translucency of the colour washes, which are used in an arbitrary, rather than a naturalistic, way. The method, though superficially recalling western watercolour practice, remains essentially oriental, but paintings of this type, of which a number of beautiful specimens were to be seen at the Arts Council exhibition of Hokusai's drawings in 1954, are among those that give the greatest pleasure to us in the west.

Another class of drawings consists of those destined for the wood-block cutter. These may be first drafts, little distinguishable from random sketches, or subsequent, more elaborated versions from which the wood-cutter's working drawing was made, either by the artist himself, or by someone working in the craftsman's workshop. Few drawings in this final form exist, since most were destroyed when the block was cut. Occasionally, however, tracings must have been made, since drawings exist that were made for the

Mangwa, the *Suikoden* (Figs. 88, 91), and other books and broadsheets. Others, again, have survived because the prints for which they were designed were never engraved: several such exist, for instance, made for the 'One Hundred Poems Explained by the Nurse' series. A few of this series of drawings, like the 'Bringing in Osiers' in the British Museum (Fig. 90), reveal the master's touch, but in many, the brushwork is too staid, or too clumsy, to be his.

But in any case, these drawings for prints are usually prepared with studied care with the eventual engraving in mind, and Hokusai's native genius for sketching is no more to be found in them than Turner's is in the drawings made for the steel-engravers. The drawings we admire most are those where Hokusai has picked up his brush to record some incident in the roadway, a particular movement of a single figure or a picturesque grouping of a crowd, or to note casually a spray of flowers or the flight of a bird; or to conjure up at the tip of his brush some of the legendary heroes and phantoms that filled his head. The title page of one of Hokusai's books shows an artist who is not content to paint with brushes held in either hand but who holds them in his mouth and feet too. The figure might be the caricature of Hokusai: it illustrates his dexterity, his colossal output, his readiness to record with all his faculties the world around him (page 8).

It is, I suppose, this wide sympathy for all forms of life in all kinds of surroundings, expressed in a medium we recognize as our own, that gives Hokusai's drawings that universality already remarked upon. Hokusai's affinity with artists of the west was recognized in an exhibition at the Stedelyk Museum in Amsterdam in 1951 of drawings by Rembrandt, Hokusai and Van Gogh.

There one could see upon the same walls, Rembrandt's 'Tobias blinded' and 'Simeon in the Temple', Hokusai's drawings of a coolie outside a refreshment house, a Chinese philosopher on his knees, and two toads, and some of Van Gogh's most characteristic landscapes in pen-and-ink.

And the cataloguer of this exhibition was reminded of the 'sense of the deeper rhythm of life' which Mr. Basil Gray considered we might find in the work of Hokusai,[1] and felt that the self-same rhythm could be sensed running through the drawings of Rembrandt and Van Gogh.

[1]Introduction to the Catalogue of the Exhibition of the Work of Hokusai at the British Museum, 1948.

94. Cock and chick.
Brush decoration for a fan. Signed Zen Hokusai Taitō. *About 1816.*
British Museum.

95. The road to the mountain. *Brush-painting. Signed Zen Hokusai I-itsu. About 1832.* Hakone Gallery, Japan.

CHAPTER SEVEN

INTERPRETATION OF POETRY·THE HUNDRED VIEWS OF FUJI·THE HUNDRED POEMS EXPLAINED BY THE NURSE

1830-1849

Towards the end of that period of inspired activity that saw the production of the great landscapes and *kwachō* series, Hokusai designed a set of prints in the *kakemono-ye* format illustrative of the 'Imagery of the Poets of China and Japan' that in some ways represents his crowning achievement in imaginative illustration hand-in-hand with emotive composition. In them, he arrives at last at what we feel to be a perfect balance between the figures and their setting.

It must have been evident from the illustrations already given that Hokusai (and, in fact, most Japanese artists), rarely made any attempt to keep strictly to the text they were illustrating. Their pictures were more often than not a gloss to the written word, explaining and extending the drift of story or poem. If we think of our own school of illustrators of the 1860s, we find that, in general, artists like Millais, Sandys, Keene and Gilbert gave as literal an interpretation as they could of the scene selected for illustration, with a wealth of apposite detail in costume and surroundings. Only in Rossetti, perhaps, was there an endeavour to illustrate in an oblique way by drawing out the overtones of the poem rather than stressing its more obvious import. Hokusai, at times, took as many liberties with the text of a poem as he did with the contours of a landscape, the result partly of his own capricious reaction to the subject-matter of the book he was illustrating, and partly of the underlying considerations of formal arrangement within the framework of his design. The incident in a poem was taken as a *point de départ,* not used as an anchor.

The 'Imagery of the Poets' and, to a lesser degree, the later series 'One Hundred Poems Explained by the Nurse' exemplify Hokusai's genius for this kind of free translation from one art to another, translation that conveys the spirit of the text rather than a literal word-for-word interpretation. In the 'Imagery of the Poets', no actual poems to which the pictures can be allied are given on the print, the name of the poet affording the only clue to the artist's intent. Such a method presupposed a profound knowledge in the beholder of both Japanese and Chinese anthologies, and destroys completely the notion that the Yedo print-buyers were people without culture.

Sometimes Hokusai depicts the poet in an actual or semi-legendary event from the poet's life, and sometimes one or even more of his poems are suggested. A consideration in detail of two or three of the ten prints forming the set will make the subtlety and profundity of his interpretations evident.

Tōru-no-Daijin (Fig. 96) a ninth-century prince and poet, was famed for his prodigality, especially for the moonlight revels held in the grounds of his fabulous palace at Rokujō, Kyōto, where he and his friends composed their poetry. He is depicted in the Court dress of the time, with a fan over one shoulder, declaiming his lines to two retainers in a lakeshore scene under the magic of the sickle moon, a moon that was thought to be a lucky sight on its third evening. What were the verses that held his audience spellbound? Hokusai hints, probably, at two poems, one from the best-known of the Japanese anthologies, the *Hyakunin Isshu* ('One Poem from each

96. Tōru-no-Daijin declaiming poetry before
admiring retainers.
From the set 'The Imagery of the Poets of China and Japan'.

a curving hook: the birds that fly in the clouds above in their panic mistake it for a bow.' Those for whom the print was intended would not have failed to find a wealth of allusion: the crescent moon first, then the lake of Tōru's Palace, man-made to resemble Shiogama Bay; and, for the subtlest, the link between this imitation Bay and Tōru's Japanese poem, in which the printed fabrics are those of Michinoku (Mutsu), the Province containing Shiogama Bay.

The waterfall print in this series is dedicated to Ri Haku (Li Po, the most famous of the Chinese Poets) (Plate XVI). It shows the aged poet in rapt admiration of the waterfall, oblivious of his precarious position, and only prevented from falling into the abyss by the kindly ministrations of two young acolytes. With this touch, Hokusai refers to the divine intoxication habitual in the poet. The poem most likely to have been in the artist's mind is no doubt that concerning the Waterfall of Lo-Shan in Kaing-si, most beautifully translated by Shigeyoshi Obata:

> As wind-driven snow speed the waters
> Like a white rainbow spanning the dark.
> I wonder if Heaven's River (the Milky
>   Way) has fallen from above
> To course through the mid-sky of clouds.
> Long I lift my gaze. Oh, prodigious force!
> How majestic the creation of Gods!

The 'Waterfalls' series of prints may have prepared us for the originality of this composition, in which the sheer column of striated blues pours down from top to bottom of the page, its uncompromising verticality broken by the projecting cliffs left and right: but the effective balance struck between the group formed by the poet and his attendants and the waterfall, the human element holding its own against the elemental forces of nature, however immense and awesome, figures and landscape integrated into a design of singular intensity, this is the especial triumph of the 'Ri Haku' print.

Others in the series are equally successful,

of One-hundred Poets'), a poem in which Tōru-no-Daijin likens the maze of his thoughts as a lover to the intricate patterns of certain famous printed fabrics; and the other a Chinese poem by Tōru on the crescent moon, translated by Mr. Arthur Waley:[1] 'The fish that wander in the water suspect that it is

---

[1] Binyon and Sexton, *Japanese Colour Prints.*

97. Toba exiled. *From the same set as last.*

98. 'Gathering Rushes'. *From the same set as last.*

the 'Toba' (Fig. 97) with its image of the exiled Chinese calligraphist gazing forlornly on a winter scene in an alien land being one of the most moving of any of Hokusai's prints; the *Tokusa Kari* ('Gathering Rushes' [Fig. 98] the title of a Nō play) is perhaps the most poetic of any of his moonlight landscapes. Withal, there is a seriousness, an evocativeness, that makes this set of prints one of the artist's most memorable works.

About the same time, the set of five prints usually called the 'Goblins' was issued. Phantoms and goblins were a constant preoccupation with Hokusai; they seem to have been no less real to him, with the incurably superstitious mind of the Japanese, than they were to Europeans of the Dark Ages. Japanese art and literature are full of revenants, they occur with unfailing regularity in novels and legends as instruments of revenge, that prime theme of so many Japanese stories. Having laid our ghosts long ago, we find something a

99. Cranes on a snowy pine.
Signed Zen *Hokusai I-itsu.*
About 1830.

the offerings laid before the deceased's memorial tablet (Fig. 100); a skeleton of a murdered man pulls aside, with bony hand, the mosquito curtain around the murderer's bed; a lantern changes by a sinister metamorphosis into the skull of Oiwa, to terrorize her husband when he visits the grave with his second wife (Fig. 101). The colour-printing process was never used with greater finesse than in this series. The quality of printing and engraving, as the reproduction of the serpent shows, was of an almost incredible refinement.

To these same years, just before and after 1830, belong five *kakemono-ye* of an amplitude, an urbanity, that stamps them as the work of a consummate master. They are not connected by any title, but by the uniformity of the size and the type of subject naturally form a group apart. There is a falcon among plum-blossom; turtles swimming; cranes among snow-laden branches (Fig. 99); two carp, one ascending a cascade, the other falling; and two horses and a foal. These prints, especially the last, are among the greatest rarities of Hokusai's engraved work. They are of the same order as the 'Large Flowers' but more ambitious in scope, challenging by their very format the paintings of the masters of *kwachō*, and recalling the splendours of the richly-coloured paintings of Yeitoku and Chokuan, and other great animal and bird artists of the past.

The last set of landscape designs to be issued in broadsheet form was that entitled *Chiye no Umi,* 'The Ocean of One Thousand Pictures'. These prints are still signed *Zen Hokusai I-itsu,* a name in use until 1833, after which Manji and Gwakyō Rōjin (Old Man Mad about Drawing) were used. Although of small size, each of the prints comprising the set (the series comprises ten prints in all) is extremely dramatic in composition and colour. Hokusai has given point each time to the event he is recording by emphasis upon elements in the design, and on contrasts of colour, that turn everyday happenings into

little naïve in the constant depictions of wraiths and phantoms, but this particular set of five (all that were performed of a set originally intended to be much larger if their title *Hyaku Monogatari,* 'The Hundred Ghost Stories', is any guide), are such as to make our blood run cold despite our sophisticated disbelief. A ghost appears as a snake among

100. A serpent entwining itself around a memorial tablet and gift offerings for the dead.
One of a set of five entitled 'The Hundred Tales'.

101. Oiwa's ghost. *From the same set as last.*

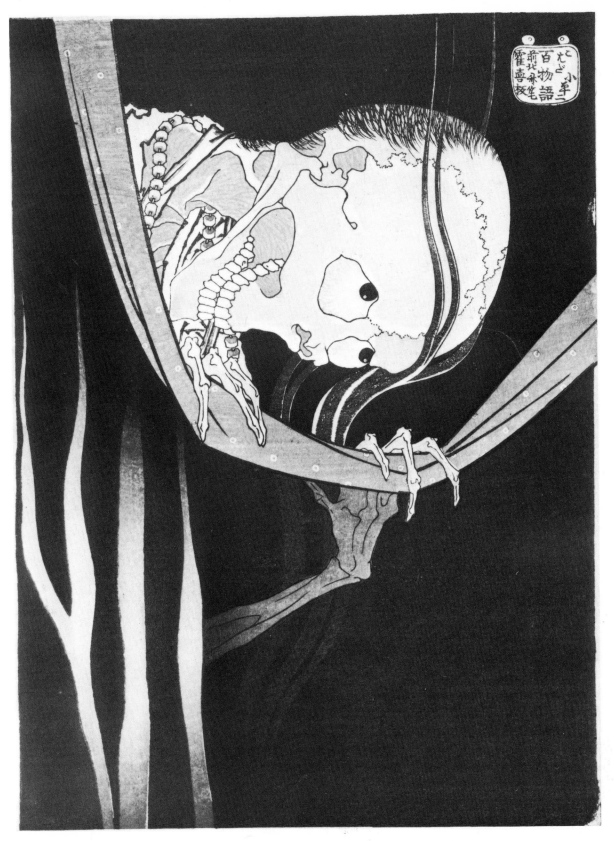

102. The ghost of Kohada Kohei returns to haunt her murderer. *From the same set as last.*

103. The grinning Hannya, a demon in a Nō play. *From the same set as last.*

fantasies. The whale landed off the Gotō Islands is made unimaginably monstrous by the juxtaposition of a flotilla of Lilliputian boats, and the intense black of its hide in a landscape of soft hues picks out its grotesque shape, and makes the area of threshed water in which it struggles the focal point to a design that eddies about it (Plate XVII). In another, two little fishing boats are adrift off the coast of Chishi, and in this Hokusai gives one of his most daring representations of a rough sea, the whole design being composed of one great precipitous cliff of foaming water that floods over the page, and the awful hollow beneath it. Another is a night-piece, the sky an intense black pricked with stars, and men fishing, brandishing brilliant flares. Prints of this set are also among the rarest of Hokusai's and fortunate indeed is the collector who owns any of them in fine state, for they represent the artist in inimitable vein.

With these, other equally rare prints should be mentioned, the designs for fans, which by their very nature are the least likely of any prints to survive. One or two of the finest are reproduced in the Paris Exhibition Catalogue of 1913 and of those, that of the 'Cocks and Hens' is one of the most superb even of Hokusai's wonderful array of bird designs.

The years subsequent to 1830 are memorable for some of Hokusai's finest books, the anthology of Chinese poems of the T'ang period, called the *Tōshisen,* the books of 'Warriors' and the immortal 'Hundred Views of Fuji'.

The *Tōshisen* is a singular triumph for the aged Popular School idol. His three books (each of five volumes), published in 1833 and 1836, formed the seventh, eighth, and ninth parts of an immense undertaking that had begun as long ago as 1788, the earlier parts having been illustrated by painters of the Kanō or Chinese Schools. As Toda wrote:[1] 'No other Ukiyo-ye artist of the period could

work in this kind of subject, and it is doubtful whether any masters of earlier periods could draw Chinese subjects with such freedom as Hokusai. The fact that Hokusai was the only man in the Ukiyo-ye school who was able to work so well in this kind of picture shows not only his unusual ability, but also the nature of his technique, which has many Chinese elements.' One notices a rare economy of line in Hokusai's drawings, a restraint where usually there is an exuberance, and these illustrations are unquestionably the finest of the whole *Tōshisen* series (Figs. 105–6).

The three major books of 'Warriors', apart from the *Suikoden* volumes, are entitled *Yehon Sakigake* (1835) (Fig. 104), *Yehon Musashi Abumi* 'The Stirrups of Musashi' (1836), and *Yehon Wakan no Homare,* 'The Glories of China and Japan' (1837). The lore of unfamiliar legend, and the erudition in matters of weapons and accoutrements in these designs of armoured knights of outlandish lineage engaged in mortal struggles, is too recondite to interest us greatly, and the repeated mannerisms in the drawings, especially in the faces of the grimacing heroes, succeed in caricaturing strife instead of making it frightful. In the preface to the 'Stirrups of Musashi' Hokusai declares that his aim was to show the freedom of movement of the human body under heavy armour, but the bewilderingly-garbed warriors engaged in hand-to-hand tussles often present a problem picture, a tangle of many limbs that do not seem to make one complete body. These books were of unfailing popularity with the Yedo populace, embodying as they do that reverence for ancient chivalry and martial derring-do that was, and is, one of the characteristics of every Japanese man of spirit. Scattered throughout the volumes are some splendid designs that embroil the spectator in the violent events they depict and make other artists' battle-pieces seem tame beside them, only Kuniyoshi, Hokusai's young contemporary, having this faculty of seeming to make sketches in the heat of battle, trimming his brush with the

---

[1]The Ryerson Catalogue, 1931.

隠岐の次郎左門廣有
内裏にて
化鳥を退治す

104. Warrior combating a phantom in the shape of a great white bird. *From the picture book of 'Warriors'*
entitled Yehon Sakigake. *1835.*

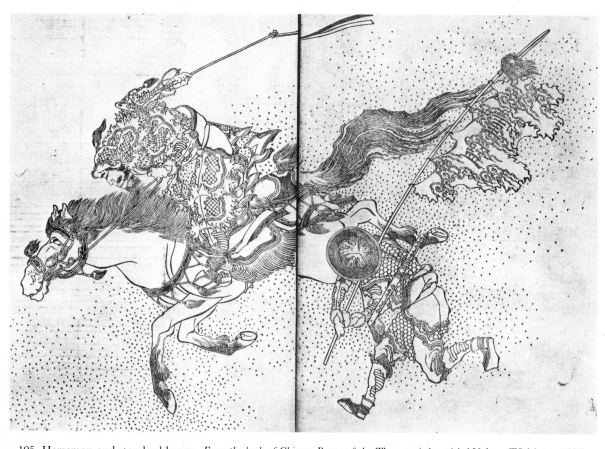

105. Horseman and standard-bearer. *From the book of Chinese Poems of the T'ang period, entitled* Yehon Tōshisen. *1833.*

XVI. Ri Haku admiring the Waterfall of Lo-Shan.
One of the set 'The Imagery of the Poets of China and Japan'. Signed Zen Hokusai I-itsu. About 1830.

XVII. Landing a whale off the Gotō Islands.
One of the set entitled Chiye no Umi, *'The Ocean of One Thousand Pictures'. About 1830–3. Signed* Zen *Hokusai I-itsu.*

XVIII. The exiled poet Nakamaro: an illustration of his poem 'O can it be that the moon I see wandering out into the wilderness of the sky is the same moon that rises over Mikasa Hill in my own Kasuga?'.
From the series 'The One Hundred Poems Explained by the Nurse'. Signed Zen *Hokusai Manji. About 1839–40.*

106. The artist contemplates his work. *From the* Yehon Tōshisen.

107. A summer shower.
From the book of 'One Hundred Views of Fuji', vol. 3.

razor-edged *katana* and dipping it in the blood of the fray.

In 1834 and 1835 were published the first two volumes of *Fugaku Hyakkei* 'One Hundred Views of Fuji'. The veneration in which Mount Fuji is held by the Japanese is something in itself outside our experience, and we miss the special significance that Hokusai's series of views had for his countrymen, thus enabled vicariously to make a Fuji-viewing pilgrimage. For us it is his virtuosity in basing design after design on the *leitmotiv* of Fuji, this time without the orchestration of full colour that accompanied the 'Thirty-six Views', with no more, in fact, than the engraved outline and flat washes of grey, that commands our admiration. In some ways, this series of 'One Hundred Views', by its exemplification of what can be achieved by ingenuity in choice of viewpoint, inventive composition, marriage of central theme with minor motifs, has had more effect upon

western art than any other of the artist's works.

Looking through the pages, we cannot fail to be impressed by the inexhaustible originality in presentation, the power to make each page, through his genius for composition, for improvisation, grip our attention as though we were looking on the depiction of something never before seen by mortal eyes, until we analyse the picture and find that it is composed of quite everyday things and only the curious or unexpected glimpse of Fuji transmutes the ordinary into the memorable (Figs. 107–13). As one of the 'Three Lucky Things' (the other two were a Falcon and an Egg-plant) and as one of the 'Three Whites' (Snow and a Crane were the others), Fuji had figured in innumerable Japanese pictures before Hokusai, but nobody had extemporized on these elements so boldly as Hokusai, who makes a design as artificial in its grouping as our engravers' imbroglios of musical instruments, but without destroying the naturalness of the scene, the impress of its actuality. However fortuitous the unexpected glimpses of Fuji may seem, it is the artist's eye that has selected them: he sees Fuji behind the hanging strips of cloth outside a dyer's premises; beyond the umbrella tops set out to dry in a maker's yard (could Renoir have been thinking of this when he painted his *Parapluies*?); through the close stems of swaying bamboo, and even, reflected, in the *sake*-cup held by a tippler. However whimsical the viewpoint may seem, the overriding consideration has been that of composition; indeed, observing the mountain from what we feel must be a unique vantage point serves only to heighten our sense of the compelling design.

It is interesting to compare this tour-de-force of Hokusai's with another artist's 'Hundred Views of Fuji', a book published in 1785 (though the artist, Minsetsu, appended a note to the effect that the drawings were made before 1765). Minsetsu's pictures are bald outline cuts of a guide-book type, that look primitive beside Hokusai's accomplished de-

108. The 'Three Whites' (Fuji, Snow and Crane). *From vol. 2 of the same book.*

109. 'The Dragon of the Storm'. *From vol. 2 of the same book. 1835.*

110. Fuji seen through a bamboo thicket. *From vol. 2 of the same book. 1835.*

111. Fuji idolatry. *From vol. 1 of the same book.*

112. Cranes and Fuji.
From vol. 1 of the same book.

113. Fuji from an umbrella-maker's yard.
From vol. 3 of the same book.

signs. In them the cone of Fuji comes forward or recedes as the scene changes, but that is the limit to the variation. There is no human interest, and no attempt to compose a picture with the elements at the artist's disposal. With Hokusai, although the landscapes have the look of views taken at random—chance vistas—every one has been skilfully chosen, but it is the manner in which he has emphasized the pattern of the scene which compels the second glance.

These three volumes proved immensely popular and passed through many editions, some of which, taken from blocks that had lost their sharp edges and no longer absorbed the ink, are travesties of the lovely prints of the first edition. Volumes 1 and 2 are to be told, apart from the excellence of the impressions, by the blind-printed salmon-coloured covers with the blue-printed title slip of a shape that has led this edition to be called the 'Falcon's Feather' edition. They represent a standard of monochrome printing that has never been excelled, even in Japan. The third volume was not dated and the only safe guide to the edition is the quality of the printing.

The last great series of prints was that entitled *Hyakunin Isshu Ubagwa Yetoki*, 'Hundred Poems Explained (or illustrated) by the Nurse', commenced about 1839. It was fitting that Hokusai should have turned to the anthology that is part of the everyday thought and speech of every Japanese except the most illiterate, and there is some suggestion in the quaint title of an old wiseacre bringing the poems within the understanding of the simplest of his audience. Yet Hokusai's interpretations are often anything but simple, sometimes the link between poem and picture is a tenuous one, apparent only to those steeped in the deeper meanings of the lines illustrated, or of the history of the poet concerned. For as in the earlier 'Imagery of the Poets', sometimes the poet is the subject of the print, sometimes the poem.

Delightful as these prints are as a whole, it is doubtful if any one of them is quite so impressive as the best of the 'Imagery of the Poets': they are accomplished to a degree that puts them far beyond the range of all but one or two of the artists living at the time but we miss in them the majestic power, the serenity, of the 'Imagery of the Poets'. Yet as colour-prints, few can fail to respond to the 'Hundred Poems'. Hokusai, or perhaps we should say, his printer, uses a fuller palette than elsewhere, and fine proofs from this set are masterpieces of the art of colour-printing as such: the print reproduced in colour (Plate XVIII) with its perfectly gradated colours in the sky and the foreground promontory, the sharply-defined and accurately registered patches of colour on the dresses, is a miracle of the art. The exiled poet Nakamaro is contemplating the reflected moon in the sea that divides him from his beloved Japan, ignoring the attendants making low obeisance, and thinking only of his native land. Hokusai is illustrating the famous lines, 'O can it be that the moon I see wandering out into the wilderness of the sky is the same moon that rises over Mikasa Hill in my own Kasuga?'. Nakamaro went to China in A.D. 716 but failed to return to Japan, one legend maintaining that the Emperor of China, suspecting his motives, detained him, drugged him with wine and left him to starve to death. Awakening, Nakamaro gazed out on the moonlit sky, bit his thumb and wrote these lines on the sleeve of his garment. Hokusai has suggested imprisonment in the screens and the guard of Chinese soldiers, but not the more improbable details of the legend.

Every one of the twenty-seven prints known of this series is full of meaning, and it is intriguing to follow in each Hokusai's treatment of the poem selected. The amorous poem of Fujiwara no Michinobu 'Though I know the morning will bring the next night nearer, yet morning is hateful to me' is illustrated by the reluctance of coolies to start their day's toil; and in another the languorous mood of men resting after a bath is made to illustrate the poem of Fujiwara no Yoshitake

114. A *daimyō* musing on a lost love. *An illustration to a poem by Sanji Hitoshi.*
One of the 'One Hundred Poems Explained by the Nurse'.

115. Women diving for Awabi off the coast of Ise. *An illustration to a poem by Sangi Takamura.*
From the same series as last.

116. The Bay of Naniwa. *An illustration to a poem by Motoyoshi Shinnō. From the same series as last.*

117. Women gathering water-lilies. *An illustration to a poem by Bunya no Asayasu. From the same series as last.*

'Once I cared not for living, now for your sake, O Love, I would life might endure for ever', but usually the interpretations are without humorous quip, though an old man's whimsies lead to an odd detail here and there. The bright and unusual contrasts of colour are quite peculiar to this set, and this, coupled with the bold conventionalized landscapes and his manneristic way of drawing the human figures, stamps these prints with an individuality unusually strong even for Hokusai (Figs. 114–17).

There were few prints after this series, indeed, for some reason or other, even drawings made for 'One Hundred Poems'

remained unengraved and are still extant. He collaborated with his young contemporaries Kuniyoshi, Shigenobu (his son-in-law), Yeisen and Kunisada in several books of poems in the years 1848 and 1849 and published a treatise on the 'Proper use of Colours' (from which an extract is given in Chapter VI) in 1848. But none of these is of first consequence. The large print of surveyors at work in an extensive landscape, drawn in the last year of his life, is evidence that Hokusai was to the last capable of providing worthwhile drawings to the publishers, but he seems to have devoted far more time in his last decade to brush-painting.

118. Chinese junk. *From the* Yehon Kanso Gundan *(1840–5), a book of dynastic wars in China.*

EPILOGUE

IT can, I think, be truthfully said of Hokusai that when he died in 1849, he died 'brush in hand', arguing sorrowfully that given ten, no, given even five years longer, he might have become a great painter. His poverty and the squalor of the hovel he lived in with his daughter Oyei, his indifference to money and the eccentricity of his behaviour towards other people, were all faithfully recorded in the *Katsushika Hokusai den* from the testimony of those who had known him in his last years. It is a picture of an old man pathetically alone with his art, who had dedicated all his days to drawing and found no time for the graces of living, remaining to the end unsociable and difficult to approach, who neither drank wine nor smoked tobacco, and who only ate enough to keep his hardy old body alive. His one driving force was the urge to draw, not, certainly, to earn an easy way of life, nor even to win renown, though he was not averse to recognition; but from an innate propensity to translate everything within his experience, the daily round of men and women, the Yedo scene, the Japanese countryside, story, legend, history and poetry, into the language of the brush, a language which we now read and enjoy and think we understand, though separated from him by an abyss of years and a way of life he could not have dreamed of. But art has no frontiers, and bridges the centuries.

A final word must be added on Hokusai's influence on painting in Japan and in the West. In Japan, a large number of artists are classified as his pupils, many of whom expressed their allegiance to him by taking an art-name related to his own, but few probably received direct instruction from him. Sōri, his earliest pupil, has already been mentioned in Chapter II. Shinsai and Gakutei were primarily *surimono* designers who worthily continued in the style formulated by the master. Hokkei, also a brilliant *surimono* artist, came nearest of any other artist to Hokusai in books of sketches recalling the *Mangwa,* and produced, as did Gakutei, at least one very individual set of landscape prints that owe little to Hokusai's exemplars. Hokuba devoted himself largely to brush-painting, in which he displayed an aristocratic touch that has brought him a certain recognition even from native connoisseurs. Hokuju was a landscapist who showed a decided leaning towards European methods of perspective and chiaroscuro and whose curious prints are much sought after for the wayward charm this odd blending of styles occasioned. Taito closely copied Hokusai's style in *kwachō* and the 'warrior' genre; so closely, in fact, that in his lifetime he earned the derisive nickname of 'Dog Hokusai'. It is no easy matter to distinguish his drawings and prints of this type from Hokusai's, and apart from Hokkei, nobody came closer to Hokusai's manner than Taito. To add to the confusion, this pupil actually forged Hokusai's signature (Zen Hokusai I-itsu) on a series of large 'Birds and Flowers' closely imitating the master's famous set, and it says much for his powers that these prints are considered little inferior to Hokusai's.

But outside his own circle, Hokusai seems to have had little influence upon his countrymen. The other most virile line of Ukiyo-ye painters was the Utagawa family, numbering among its members Toyokuni's

119. Self-portrait of Hokusai as an old man. *Brush-drawing*. Louvre, Paris.

followers, Kunisada I (known as Toyokuni III) and Kuniyoshi, two artists of great power who were able to rise, the first occasionally, the second generally, above the debased level to which colour-print production had fallen in this period of the 'decadence' of the art; and Toyohiro's pupil, Hiroshige, who designed landscapes that are among the best-loved prints of the whole Ukiyo-ye range. None of these seems to have felt the influence of Hokusai to any extent, and though occasionally Kuniyoshi's battle-pieces are reminiscent in their vitality and their pageantry of stirring events of Hokusai's books of 'Warriors', the resemblance is more due to the closeness of the two artists' subject-matter than to any desire, or need, on the part of the younger man to borrow ideas either of treatment or technique from the veteran of the rival sub-school.

And the same can be said of Hiroshige's landscapes. His most notable series, the 'Fifty-three Stations of the Tōkaidō' appeared about 1834–5, only a few years after the last of Hokusai's Fuji series had been published, but his prints rely less on the power of the brush line and more on the art of the colour-printer, more on the capture of transient atmospheric effects than on the creation of monumental design. His 'Thirty-six Views of Fuji' afford an even closer basis of comparison, but to place prints of this set beside those of Hokusai's of the same title is to realize the fundamental dissimilarity of the two artists' work, a difference that can best be expressed perhaps, by an analogy from music, the art of the older man having the controlling form of a symphony, the other the freedom of a rhapsody.

By the time of Hokusai's death in 1849, the Ukiyo-ye colour-print movement was almost a spent force. After the Revolution of 1868, an artist here and there like Kyōsai showed a flicker of the old style, but that, too, soon died out. With the embracing of westernization, all hopes of a national school of art based on the Ukiyo-ye style, either of Hokusai or anyone else, had vanished and indeed, any revival could only have been an archaistic resurrection with no hope of a prolonged life. After his early years, Hokusai broke away from the orthodox Ukiyo-ye style and created a manner of his own, and, as I have shown, had no followers of really outstanding stature and no influence of a lasting nature on the art of his countrymen. He remains, in fact, one of the great solitary figures in Japanese art.

By one of those strange interactions of the art of one country upon that of another, Hokusai's work has had a more significant influence upon Western art than upon that of his own country. Becoming widely known in Europe at a time when the traditions of conception and technique in painting were in the melting pot, and art in that malleable state when it took the impress of any alien mould provided it offered an alternative to the existing out-worn models, Hokusai's art, like that of other Japanese artists, Utamaro especially, served to reinforce the trend already noticeable in European art in the direction of a new formalism, the aim towards the creation of monumental designs from the random elements of nature. Simplification, in landscape as much as in figure painting, was in the air, and Hokusai, as the most popular and widely known of the Japanese print artists, was part of the atmosphere of change and experiment, as is proved by the admission of indebtedness to his work made by many of the French impressionists and the innovators that immediately followed them.

In a more direct way, Hokusai has been partly responsible, I think, for certain trends in book illustration and decoration, a responsibility he shares with a number of his countrymen. Of all his works, the 'Hundred Views of Fuji' has probably been the greatest force in this direction. To appreciate its effect upon western illustration, one cannot do better than to recall the state of that by-product of the art of our own country in the year 1880, when F. W. Dickins wrote a commentary on Hokusai's great book and the three volumes were reprinted, imperfectly it is true, but sufficiently well for the purpose; and then to imagine the impact of these Fuji engravings upon a public used to the pictorial inanities of the monthly magazines and illustrated novels of the time, printed from engraved wood-blocks, like Hokusai's designs, but what a world apart from the Japanese master's imaginatively designed and superbly engraved pages! How many artists, and artists to be, brought up in the Victorian tradition of book illustration, must have been stirred to their depths as they turned page after page of these incomparable designs, marvelling at the originality, the fecundity, the virtuosity, the revelation of immense vistas newly opened to them.

It may be difficult to point to specific examples of a direct influence of Hokusai in the generation that saw, and followed, the publication of Dickins's book, but like the rest of Hokusai's work that was by that time reaching the west, it proved an inspiration that widened the vision rather than a model to be copied, with an effect the more incalculable because it was so fundamental and profound.

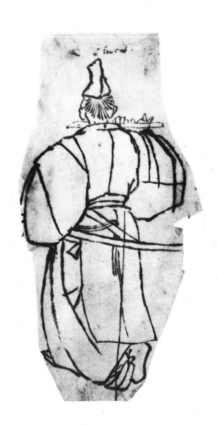

SHORT GLOSSARY OF JAPANESE WORDS

BIJIN-YE. Pictures of beautiful girls.

BON (or HON). Book.

DAIMYŌ. The lord of a Province.

DERA (or TERA). A temple.

FUDE. A writing or painting brush; an artist's brush-work.

FŪRYŪ. Fashionable, *à la mode*.

FUSUMA. Sliding partitions in Japanese rooms.

GEISEI. Art-surname.

GŌ. Art-name, *nom de pinceau*.

GWA. Picture or drawing; drawn by.

GWAFU. Sketchbook.

GWAJŌ. Folding album with pictures.

GWAMYŌ. Art personal name.

HAIKAI. Seventeen-syllable poems.

HAKKEI. Eight views forming a series.

HAN. Engraved block for printing.

HASHIRA. Inscription on the outer edges of a book, giving title, page number, etc.

HASHIRAKAKE. Pillar-hanging print, about 27 in. by 4 in.

HASHIRA-YE. Same as HASHIRAKAKE.

HIBACHI. A pan holding charcoal for warming purposes.

HON (or BON). Book.

HONYA. Bookshop; bookseller.

HOSO-YE. Narrow vertical print, about 12 in. by 6 in.

HYAKUNIN ISSHU. Anthology of the One Hundred Poets, made, according to tradition, in the thirteenth century.

HYAKU. One hundred.

ICHIMAI-YE. Single-sheet prints.

KABUKI. Dramatic performances; the Popular theatre.

KAKEMONO. A hanging picture.

KAKEMONO-YE. A print in kakemono form, usually about 27 in. by 12 in.

KAMURO. Girl attendant of OIRAN, the principal courtesan.

KENTŌ. Guide-mark on wood-blocks for securing accurate register.

KIBYŌSHI. 'Yellow-backs', small story books.

KIWAME. Approved (by the censor).

KWACHŌ-YE. Pictures of flowers and birds.

KYŌKA. Comic verses of 31 syllables.

MEISHO (or MEISHO-KI). Guide-book.

MON. Badge or device denoting family, house, etc.

MONOGATARI. Narrative tale, romance.

NISHIKI-YE. Brocade pictures, i.e., colour-prints.

NŌ. The classical drama.

OBI. Sash or girdle.

OIRAN. Superior class of courtesan.

OTOKODATE. One of a fraternity of chivalrous men who defended the weak and wronged against oppression.

SAMISEN. Three-stringed musical instrument.

SEIRŌ. Green-Houses, i.e., houses licensed for prostitution, e.g., Yoshiwara in Yedo.

SHINZŌ. An apprentice courtesan.

TANZAKU. Narrow vertical prints, about 14 in. by 4 in.

TOBA-YE. Comic pictures of caricature type, named after Toba Sōjō, a painter of the eleventh to twelfth centuries.

UCHIWA-YE. Print for mounting on a non-folding fan.

UKI-YE. Perspective pictures.

UKIYO-YE. Literally, Pictures of the Floating World; figuratively, Pictures of Gay Life.

YEHON. Picture-book.

YOKO-YE. Horizontal picture.

YOMI-HON. Reading book.

BIBLIOGRAPHY

DICKINS, F. W. *Fugaku hiyaku-kei, or a Hundred Views of Fuji (Fusiyama): by Hokusai.* London, 1880.

MORSE, E. 'Notes on Hokusai, the founder of the modern Japanese school of drawing.' *American Art Review*, 1880.

DURET, T. 'L'art Japonais, Hokusai.' *Gazette des Beaux-Arts*, Paris, 1882.

GONSE, L. *L'Art Japonais.* Paris, 1883.

ANDERSON, W. *Descriptive and historical catalogue of a collection of Japanese and Chinese Paintings in the British Museum.* London, 1886.

RENAN. A. 'La Mangwa d'Hokousai.' *Le Japon artistique*, Nos. 8 and 9, Paris, 1888-9.

HUISH, M. B. *Catalogue of a collection of Drawings and Engravings by Hokusai Exhibited at the Fine Art Society.* Introductory note by Marcus B. Huish. London, 1890.

GEFFROY, G. 'Hokusai à Londres.' *La Vie artistique*, 1ᵉ série, Paris, 1892.

FENOLLOSA, E. F. *Boston, Museum of Fine Arts. Department of Japanese Art. Special Exhibition of the Pictorial Art of Japan and China. No. 1. Hokusai and his School.* Boston, 1893.

IIJIMA, HANJŪRŌ. *Katsushika Hokusai den.* Tokyo, 1893.

STRANGE, E. F. *Japanese Prints and Albums of Prints in colour in the National Art Library, South Kensington.* London, 1894.

DESHAYES, E. 'Hokousai et l'école populaire au Japon.' *L'idée libre*, Paris, 1894.

GONCOURT, E. DE. *Hokousai.* Paris, 1896.

BING. S. 'La vie et l'oeuvre d'Hok'saï. L'Art japonais avant Hok'saï. La jeunesse d'Hok'saï. Shunrô.' *Revue Blanche*, Paris, 1896.

FENOLLOSA, E. F. *The Masters of Ukiyoye.* New York, 1896.

REVON, H. *Étude sur Hok'saï.* Paris, 1896.

HOLMES, C. J. *Hokusai.* London, 1899.

BING, S. 'The Thirty Six Views of Fuji.' *Transactions of the Japan Society*, London, 1899.

ASTON, W. G. *A History of Japanese Literature.* London, 1899.

DURET, T. *Catalogue des livres et albums illustrés du Japon de la Collection Duret au Cabinet des Estampes.* Paris, 1900.

FENOLLOSA, E. F. *Catalogue of the Exhibition of Paintings of Hokusai Held at Japan Fine Art Association, Uyeno Park, Tokio, from 13th to 30th January, 1900.* Tokyo, 1901.

FENOLLOSA, E. F. *An Outline of the History of Ukiyoye.* Tokyo, 1901.

PERZYNSKI, F. *Hokusai.* Bielefeld and Leipzig, 1904.

JUNGO, MURAYAMA. *On Hokusai's 'Daily Exorcisms' (Katsushika Hokusai Nisshin Mayokei Chō).* Tokyo, 1906.

STRANGE, E. F. *Hokusai. The Old Man Mad with Painting.* London, 1906.

TAJIMA, S. *Masterpieces Selected from the Ukiyoye School*, Vol. IV. Tokyo, 1908.

ROTHENSTEIN, W. *Two Drawings by Hok'saï. From the Collection of W. Rothenstein.* Broad Campden, Glos., 1910.

MORRISON, A. *The Painters of Japan.* London, 1911.

AUBERT, L. 'Hokusai.' *Revue de Paris*, 1913.

LEMOISNE, P. A. 'Yeishi, Chōki, Hokousai.' *Gazette des Beaux-Arts*, Paris, 1913.

LEBEL, J. 'Hokousai.' *Art et Décoration*, Paris, 1913.

V.I. Catalogue. Vol. V. *Yeishi, Chōki, Hokusai. Estampes Japonaises... Exposées au Musée des Arts Décoratifs en Janvier 1913.* Introduction by R. Koechlin, catalogue by Vignier, Lebel and Inada. Paris, 1913.

FOCILLON, H. *Hokousai.* Paris, 1914.

BINYON, L. A. *Catalogue of Japanese and Chinese Woodcuts in the British Museum.* London, 1916.

STEWART, B. *Subjects Portrayed in Japanese Prints.* London, 1922.

BINYON, L. and SEXTON, J. J. O'BRIEN. *Japanese Colour Prints.* London, 1923.

BROWN, L. N. *Block Printing and Book Illustration in Japan.* London, 1924.

LEDOUX, L. V. *A Descriptive Catalogue of an Exhibition of Japanese Landscape, Bird and Flower Prints, and Surimono from Hokusai to Kyōsai.* New York, The Grolier Club, 1924.

MURDOCH, J. *A History of Japan.* Vol. III. *The Tokugawa Epoch, 1652-1868.* London, 1926.

ODA, KAZUMA. *Life of Hokusai.* Tokyo, 1928.

INOUE, K. 'The relationship between Hokusai and his pupil Hokusen who took over the name Taito when Hokusai relinquished it.' *Ukiyoyeshi*, Tokyo, 1929.

SALAMAN, M. C. *Hokusai.* Masters of the Colour-Print series. London, 1930.

Ukiyo-ye Taisei. Vol. IX. Tokyo, 1930.

ODA, KAZUMA. *Ukiyo-ye to sashi-ye geijutsu* (Ukiyo-ye and the art of illustration). Tokyo, 1931.

TODA, K. *Descriptive Catalogue of Japanese and Chinese illustrated books in the Ryerson Library of the Art Institute, Chicago.* Chicago., 1931.

NOGUCHI, Y. *Hokusai.* Tokyo, 1932.

Ukiyo-ye Taika Shūsei. Vol. 15. Tokyo, 1932.

SHIBUI, KIYOSHI. *Ukiyo-ye Naishi.* Tokyo, 1932.

MIZUTANI, YUMIHIKO. *Kohan Shōsetsu Sōgwa Shi* (A History of Early Illustrated Fiction). Tokyo, 1936.

NAGASSE, TAKESHIRO. *Le Paysage dans l'art de Hokusai.* Paris, 1937.

MODDERMAN, E. J. *Japansche Teekeningen en Schetsen. Tentoonstelling in het Frans Hals Museum te Haarlem.* Haarlem, 1938.

NARAZAKI, MUNESHIGE. *Hokusai Ron* (A Discourse on Hokusai). Tokyo, 1944.

KAZUO, FUKUMOTO. *Hokusai to Inshoha no Hitobito* (Hokusai and the Impressionists). Tokyo, 1947.

TAICHIRŌ, KOBAYASHI. *Hokusai to Degas* (Hokusai and Degas). Tokyo, 1947.

GRAY, B. *British Musuem. The Work of Hokusai. Woodcuts, Illustrated Books, Drawings and Paintings: a Catalogue of an Exhibition held on the occasion of the Centenary of his Death.* Introduction by Basil Gray. London, 1948.

MILLER, KATHERINE. *Hokusai. Japanische Holzschnitte und Zeichnungen.* Zürich, 1948.

BRUIJN, R. DE. *Catalogus der Tentoonstelling van werken van Katsushika Hokusai in Nederlandse en Belgische Openbare en Particuliere Verzamelingen.* Amsterdam, 1949.

HEMPEL, R. *Hokusai 1760-1849. Tentoonstelling Stedelyk Museum.* Amsterdam, 1949.

GRUYTER, W. J. DE. *Rembrandt, Hokusai and van Gogh.* Catalogue of an Exhibition of drawings at the Stedelyk Museum, Amsterdam, Oct.–Nov. 1951. Introduction by W. Jos. de Gruyter. Amsterdam, 1951.

LEDOUX, L. V. *Japanese Prints, Hokusai and Hiroshige, in the collection of Louis V. Ledoux.* Catalogued by the owner. Princeton, 1951.

KONDŌ, ICHITARŌ. *Hokusai.* Tokyo, 1953.

GRUYTER, W. J. DE. *Hokusai, Drawings and Water-Colours.* Catalogue of the Arts Council of Great Britain Exhibition, 1954. Introduction by W. Jos. de Gruyter. London, 1954.

WINZINGER, F. *Hokusai*, Munich, 1954.

BOLLER, W. *Hokusai.* Stuttgart, 1955.

HLOUCHA, JOE. *Hokusai.* Prague, 1955.

KONDŌ, ICHITARŌ. *Katsushika Hokusai.* English adaptation by Elise Grill. Rutland, Vt., and Tokyo, 1955.

MEISTER, P. W. *Hokusai, Handzeichnungen und Aquarellen.*

Exhibition at Hamburg Museum für Kunst und Gewerbe. Introduction by Dr. P. W. Meister. Hamburg, 1955.

GRUYTER, W. J. DE. *Hokusai.* An exhibition at Stedelyk van Abbe-Museum, Eindhoven. Introduction by W. Jos. de Gruyter. Eindhoven, 1956.

HILLIER, J. 'Hokusai: some drawings and problems of attribution.' *The Connoisseur,* London, May, 1956.

SADAO, KIKUCHI. *Hokusai.* Tokyo, 1957.

TOMITA, KOJIRŌ. *Day and Night in the Four Seasons by Hokusai.* Museum of Fine Arts, Boston, 1957.

DICKINS, F. W. *One Hundred Views of Fuji.* Introduction by J. Hillier. New York, 1958.

HILLIER, J. *Hokusai: dessins, aquarelles, estampes, livres.* An exhibition at the gallery of Huguette Berès, Paris, Introduction by J. Hillier. Paris, 1958.

MICHENER, JAMES A. *The Hokusai Sketchbooks: Selections from the Manga.* Rutland, Vt., and Tokyo, 1958.

SWANN, P. C. *Hokusai.* London, 1959.

TERRY, CHARLES S. *Hokusai's Thirty-six Views of Mt. Fuji.* Tokyo, 1959.

BOWIE, THEODORE R. 'Hokusai and the Comic Tradition in Japanese Painting.' *College Art Journal,* New York, Spring, 1960.

HILLIER, J. 'Hokusai drawings in the Harari Collection.' *The Connoisseur,* 145, London, June, 1960.

NARAZAKI, MUNESHIGE. 'Hokusai Hiroshige' in *Nihon Hangwa Bijutsu Zenshū,* Vol. V, Tokyo, 1960.

(STERN, HAROLD P.) *Hokusai Paintings and Drawings in the Freer Gallery of Art, Washington.* Washington, 1960.

CONNOR, R. *Hokusai.* Hanover, 1962.

FONTEIN, J. *Het Landschap bij Hokusai.* An exhibition at the Rijksprintenkabinet, Amsterdam. Introduction by Jan Fontein, Amsterdam, 1962.

SADAO, KIKUCHI. *Exhibition of Hokusai's Masterpieces (Sakai Collection).* Introduction by Kikuchi Sadao. New York, 1962.

Ukiyo-ye Geijutsu (Ukiyo-e Art). Edited by Nihon Ukiyo-e Kyokai. Tokyo, 1962 ff.

BIEDERMAN, EMILY. 'Some Early Prints by Hokusai in the Museum of Fine Arts, Boston.' *Bulletin,* Vol. LXI, No. 324. Boston, 1963.

SUZUKI, JŪZŌ. *Ningen Hokusai.* Tokyo, 1963.

BOWIE, THEODORE R. *The Drawings of Hokusai.* Bloomington, Ind., 1964.

KANEKO, FUSUI. *Hokusai-Ō Shinrabanshō Gwashū.* Vol. 3 of series *Ukiyo-ye Nikuhitsu Gwashū* (Ukiyo-ye Brush-paintings). Tokyo, 1964.

Tokyo National Museum Illustrated Catalogues. *Ukiyo-ye Prints* (3). Tokyo, 1964.

WINZINGER, F. 'Ein unbekennter Fächer des Hokusai.' *Pantheon,* Munich, 1965.

HILLIER, J. *Hokusai Drawings.* London, 1966.

SHŪDŌ, OZAKI. *Hokusai.* Exhibition organized by Nihon Keizai Shimbun. Introduction by Ozaki Shūdō. Tokyo, 1967.

HAYASHI, YOSHIKAZU. *Empon Kenkyū: Hokusai* (Study of Erotic Books: Hokusai). Tokyo, 1968.

HILLIER, J. *Hokusai Drawings.* An exhibition at the Anthony d'Offay Fine Art Gallery. Introduction by J. Hillier. London, 1968.

NARAZAKI, MUNESHIGE. *Masterworks of Ukiyo-e. The Thirty-six Views of Mt. Fuji.* English translation by John Bester. Tokyo, 1968.

KANEKO, FUSUI. *Nikuhitsu Katsushika Hokusai Ten.* An exhibition of Hokusai's brush-paintings at Gotō Fine Arts Museum. Text by Fusui Kaneko. Tokyo, 1969.

LONGSTREET, STEPHEN. *The Drawings of Hokusai.* Alhambra, Ca., 1969.

NARAZAKI, MUNESHIGE. *Masterworks of Ukiyo-e. Hokusai: Sketches and Paintings.* English translation by John Bester. Tokyo, 1969.

BRUIJN, R. DE. 'The one hundred poems explained by the nurse' in *The Fascinating World of the Japanese Artist.* The Hague, 1971.

SUZUKI, JŪZŌ, and others. *Hokusai Yomihon Sashiye Shūsei* (Compendium of Hokusai's Illustrations to Novels). 5 vols. Tokyo, 1971–3.

YASUDA, GOZŌ. *Gwakyō Hokusai.* Tokyo, 1971.

HILLIER, J. *Hokusai. Prints, Paintings, Drawings and Illustrated Books.* An exhibition arranged by R. G. Sawers at the Hugh Moss Ltd. Gallery. Introduction by J. Hillier. London, 1972.

Hokusai Kenkyū (Hokusai studies). Various authors. Tokyo, 1972 ff.

SUZUKI, JŪZŌ; KEYES, ROGER T. AND MORSE, PETER. *Zaigai Hihō: Hokusai* (Treasures in Foreign Collections: Hokusai). Gakken Series. Tokyo, 1972.

HILLIER, J. 'Hokusai: Enlarging the Inner Circle.' *The Stanford Museum,* Vol. II, Stanford, Ca., 1973.

BONICATTI, MAURIZIO. *Hokusai. Hiroshige.* Rome, 1974.

FORRER, MATTHI. *Hokusai. A Guide to the Serial Graphics.* Philadelphia and London, 1974.

OKA, ISABURŌ and Others. *Hokusai. Ukiyo-ye Taikei,* Vol. 8. Tokyo, 1974 and (reduced format) Tokyo, 1975.

SADAO, KIKUCHI. *Edo no Ukiyo-yeshi: Utamaro, Sharaku, Hokusai, Hiroshige.* Riccar Collection exhibition, introduction by Kikushi Sadao. Tokyo, 1975.

LANE, RICHARD. *Hokusai and Hiroshige.* Tokyo, 1976.

PETERNOLLI, GIOVANNI. 'La Fortuna Critica di Hokusai in Francia nel XIX secolo.' *Paragone,* Florence, 1976.

SCHNEEBERGER, P.-F. *Hokusai et le Japonisme avant 1900.* Geneva, 1976.

SADAO, KIKUCHI. *Gakyōjin Hokusai Ten.* An exhibition at the Kyoto City Art Museum. Text by Kikuchi Sadao. Kyoto, 1977.

LANE, RICHARD. *Hokusai and Hiroshige.* Limited edition, text in English and Japanese. Tokyo, Baltimore, Cologne, 1976.